THE
MODERN
FUNDAMENTALS
OF GOLF

BEN HOGAN

With Herbert Warren Wind

The Modern Fundamentals of Golf

Drawings by Anthony Ravielli

Pan Books
in association with Heinemann

First published 1957 by Nicholas Kaye Ltd
This edition published 1988 by Pan Books Ltd,
Cavaye Place, London SW10 9PG
© Ben Hogan 1957
All rights reserved
ISBN 0 330 30198 5
Printed and bound in Great Britain by
Biddles Ltd, Guildford

Foreword

The yearning to play a better game of golf is a national mania in America. No man who golfs is so stubborn, so conceited, so arrogant or so accomplished that he is not constantly striving to improve his score. He may not admit this to others. He may pretend that mediocrity is enough for him. ("I shoot in the 90s and I have a lot of fun. That's good enough for me.")

This man is telling a white lie and he knows it. He wants desperately to break 90 and when he does, he will want just as desperately to break 80. Let him shoot in the high 70s and he will have but one dream: par or better. Only a few days ago I played a round with a famous pro, an especially serene companion and one of the enduring masters of golf. He was on that day trying out a new set of woods for the first time. He was as happy and uninhibited as a small boy with these new tools of his trade. In the warm glow of his infectious enthusiasm I asked myself, why? Presently it dawned on me. Because they were going to make it possible for him to improve his game.

The golfer truly believes in long engagements. He courts a mistress as fickle as she is bewitching. She leads him on with little favors that fill him with hopes of conquest. Then she scorns him and humiliates him (in front of his friends, too) and leaves him despairing. Sometimes he hides his despair in rages: he hurls clubs into water hazards and presents a dozen new balls to his caddy. He is through, finished, *kaput*.

He comes back, of course. And then, suddenly the miracle happens. The despairing man who could do nothing right now can do nothing wrong. He fishes his clubs out of the water and buys the balls back from the caddy. He feels, as the song says, "now at last I know the secret of it all."

The bewitcher leads him on. Now he becomes arrogant and conceited again. He sees things clearly. He is Murder, Incorporated off the tees, sudden death on his approaches, a veritable Willie Hoppe for accuracy on the greens. In his great joy, he finds he loves all his fellow men, especially those in his own foursome. He wants to share his newly discovered secrets. He gives them freely to his companions. He is a Daddy Warbucks for generosity. He is also a pain in the neck.

But the game, the bewitcher, will take care of him. At the moment when his confidence is highest, his happiness indescribable, she will let him have it. He will slice his drive, he will blunder his way back onto the fairway and into a trap, he will four-putt the green. He will be chastened. He will know humility again.

Humility—that is the magic word. Golf is man's most humbling diversion. It may be, for that reason alone, the greatest game he has ever devised. No man—champion, top professional or President of the United States—ever reaches that point at which he can say: I have learned the secret, I have conquered the bewitcher. As I write this, there is an Associated Press dispatch before me. It quotes Ben Hogan himself as saying on the eve of a tournament: "I am trying to play myself back in shape. I just haven't had enough competition. I'm hitting the ball as well as I ever did, but I've lost the knack of scoring." Even Ben Hogan!

But if ever a man has truly learned the secret of good, of great golf, it is Ben Hogan. He has devoted his life to the game. He has studied it as few others have. He has found a way to share his knowledge with others. This, of course, as the Associated Press reported above, does not excuse Ben from constant practice—any more than a Heifitz could allow himself to forget his violin between concerts.

It has been SPORTS ILLUSTRATED's privilege to bring this master's fundamental wisdom to a wide audience by teaming him with the No. 1 golf writer of the nation, Herbert Warren Wind, and an artist with a special gift for freezing action into vivid instructional pictures, Anthony Ravielli.

This team—Hogan, Wind, Ravielli—has produced what I believe to be a classic of golf instruction. It cannot fail to improve the game of anyone who puts it to work for him. That is not my opinion alone. Thousands of golfers who have read the text and studied the illustrations during the serialization in SPORTS ILLUSTRATED have mailed in delighted (and unsolicited) testimonials. The Hogan-Wind-Ravielli prescription works. It even worked for me, a humbled and hopeful editor.

Sidney L. James
Managing Editor
Sports Illustrated

PUBLISHER'S NOTE

No attempt has been made to modify the text of this book for British readers. The view has been taken that this world-famous American golfer should be allowed to speak direct to his audience in his own idiom.

Preface

The first of the five articles comprising "The Modern Fundamentals of Golf" appeared in the March 11 issue of *Sports
Illustrated*, just about ten months after work on the project
was started. It would be wrong to give the impression that
those ten months represented uninterrupted labor and that
Ben forsook his business and his golf over that stretch in
order to devote priority attention to the articles. It went more
like this: an initial period in which Ben established the con-
tent and in which the general form of presentation was
arrived at; a second period of gestation and review on Ben's
part during which time Tony Ravielli worked out his rough
sketches and the rough drafts of the "text" were written;
and then the real work, four solid months of getting the series
into its final form, a stretch in which, after a decently calm
beginning, Ravielli worked round the clock to complete his
wonderful drawings and Ben uprooted his schedule almost
daily so that he could consider and check with his character-
istic thoroughness the correctness of every drawing and
every phrase. I recount this because teaching anything via
the printed page is no easy matter, and all of us are agreed
that the considerable success the series enjoyed—and which,
in fact, prompted its publication in more permanent form—

was due in a very large part to the unglamorous provision of enough time to approach the job properly.

Of course, the fundamental reason for the series' extraordinary popularity was a simple one: with the number of American golfers annually becoming larger and their fanaticism more intense, the time was ripe for some original and authentically progressive investigation of that bitter-sweet mystery of life, the golf swing—especially if that investigation were conducted by Ben Hogan, the greatest golfer of his time. "The Modern Fundamentals of Golf", as Ben says, represent a sifting of the knowledge he has acquired during his three decades in the game. Although golf makes a student out of anyone who touches it, it is really quite doubtful if any player throughout golf's long history has ever brought to his studies the basic tenacity, the acute and brilliantly ordered method, and the hours of relentless exploration that have marked Ben Hogan's efforts to understand the game as clearly as possible in order to be able to play it as well as possible.

It has in all ways been an extremely pleasant and rewarding collaboration for those of us who were privileged to work with Ben. My only personal regret is that my friends' golf games have improved as much as my own.

Herbert Warren Wind
May, 1957

Contents

The Fundamentals
page **13**

1. The Grip
page **18**

2. Stance and Posture
page **37**

3. The First Part of the Swing
page **61**

4. The Second Part of the Swing
page **84**

5. Summary and Review
page **109**

The Fundamentals

Twenty-five years ago, when I was 19, I became a professional golfer. I suppose that if I fed the right pieces of data
to one of our modern "electronic brain" machines it would
perform a few gyrations and shortly afterwards inform me
as to how many hundreds of thousands of shots I have hit on
practice fairways, how many thousands of shots I have
struck in competition, how many times I have taken three
putts when there was absolutely no reason for doing so, and
all the rest of it. Like most professional golfers, I have a
tendency to remember my poor shots a shade more vividly
than the good ones—the one or two per round, seldom more,
which come off exactly as I intend they should.

However, having worked hard on my golf with all the
mentality and all the physical resources available to me, I
have managed to play some very good shots at very important
stages of major tournaments. To cite one example which
many of my friends remember with particular fondness—
and I, too, for that matter—in 1950 at Merion, I needed a 4
on the 72nd to tie for first in the Open. To get that 4 I needed
to hit an elusive, well-trapped, slightly plateaued green from
about 200 yards out. There are easier shots in golf. I went
with a two-iron and played what was in my honest judgment
one of the best shots of my last round, perhaps one of the best

I played during the tournament. The ball took off on a line for the left-center of the green, held its line firmly, bounced on the front edge of the green, and finished some 40 feet from the cup. It was all I could have asked for. I then got down in two putts for my 4, and this enabled me to enter the playoff for the title which I was thankful to win the following day.

I bring up this incident not for the pleasure of retasting the sweetness of a "big moment" but, rather, because I have discovered in many conversations that the view I take of this shot (and others like it) is markedly different from the view most spectators seem to have formed. They are inclined to glamorize the actual shot since it was hit in a pressureful situation. They tend to think of it as something unique in itself, something almost inspired, you might say, since the shot was just what the occasion called for. I don't see it that way at all. I didn't hit that shot then—that late afternoon at Merion. I'd been practicing that shot since I was 12 years old. After all, the point of tournament golf is to get command of a swing which, the more pressure you put on it, the better it works.

In some important respects, tournament golf and golf are as foreign to each other as ice hockey and tennis. In other respects they're not: the professional shooting for his livelihood on the circuit (with his pride, some pleasure, and thousands of dollars at stake) and the average golfer trying to produce his best game on weekends (with his pride, his pleasure, and a dollar Nassau at stake) are both searching to master the movements that will result in a repeating swing—A CORRECT, POWERFUL, REPEATING SWING. This can be stated categorically: it is utterly impossible for any golfer to play good golf without a swing that will repeat.

How then do you build a swing that you can depend on to repeat in all kinds of wind and weather, under all kinds of presses and pressure? Having devoted the bulk of my waking hours (and a few of my sleeping hours) for a quarter of a century to the pursuit of the answer, I now believe that what

I have learned can be of tremendous assistance to all golfers. That is my reason for undertaking this series of lessons. I do not propose to deal in theory. What I have learned I have learned by laborious trial and error, watching a good player do something that looked right to me, stumbling across something that felt right to me, experimenting with that something to see if it helped or hindered, adopting it if it helped, refining it sometimes, discarding it if it didn't help, sometimes discarding it later if it proved undependable in competition, experimenting continually with new ideas and old ideas and all manner of variations until I arrived at a set of fundamentals that appeared to me to be right because they accomplished a very definite purpose, a set of fundamentals which proved to me they were right because they stood up and produced under all kinds of pressure. To put it briefly, the information I will be presenting is a sifting of the knowledge I've tried to acquire since I first met up with golf when I was 12 and knew, almost immediately, I wanted to make the game my lifework.

Up to a considerable point, as I see it, there's nothing difficult about golf, nothing. I see no reason, truly, why the average golfer, if he goes about it intelligently, shouldn't play in the 70s—and I mean by playing the type of shots a fine golfer plays. Somehow most average golfers get it into their head that they can't play a "long shot" correctly, that they haven't got the skill or coordination to execute a full swing. Putting or chipping, that's another story. The average golfer feels he can cope pretty successfully with those parts of the game—all they require is a short swing. In my opinion, the average golfer underrates himself. He has all the physical equipment he needs to execute the full golf swing and hit full shots. A full swing is nothing more or less than an extension of the short swing. Like everything, it takes some learning, but learning the correct movements is 10 times less difficult than he thinks. In fact, once you are on the right track in golf, doing things the right way takes a lot less effort than the wrong way does.

I realize that in some ways I can be a demanding man and that some things are harder for certain people to do than I may appreciate, but it really cuts me up to watch some golfer sweating over his shots on the practice tee, throwing away his energy to no constructive purpose, nine times out of 10 doing the same thing wrong he did years and years back when he first took up golf. This sort of golfer obviously loves the game or he wouldn't be out there practicing it. I cannot watch him long. His frustration—all that fruitless expenditure of energy—really bothers me. If he stands out there on the practice tee till he's 90, he's not going to improve. He's going to get worse and worse because he's going to get his bad habits more and more deeply ingrained. I know that thousands of golfers console themselves with the game's being an avenue to exercise and companionship—which is wonderful—but every golfer, at the bottom of his heart, wants to play the game relatively well. To do that takes some application, some thought, some effort, but the golfer who goes about this wisely will play good golf and should go on to enjoy his golf increasingly the rest of his life. The greatest pleasure is obtained by improving.

Before we commence the instruction, let me tell you more specifically what we will be doing and what we hope to accomplish. To begin with, the book will comprise five lessons. In each one we will be presenting the golfer-reader with one or two fundamentals for him to practice and become well acquainted with so that he will be building a progressively sound foundation on which the ensuing fundamentals can be added. The golfer who devotes a half hour daily to practicing the points we will be bringing out during these five lessons will, I believe, improve his game and his scoring immediately and decisively. The degree of improvement his game will show will vary with the quality of each individual's application. By continuing to practice and apply these fundamentals, the golfer will continue to improve his game—quite often, far beyond his fondest dreams. I do genuinely believe this: THE AVERAGE GOLFER IS EN-

TIRELY CAPABLE OF BUILDING A REPEATING SWING AND BREAKING 80, if he learns to perform a small number of correct movements and conversely, it follows, eliminates a lot of movements which tend to keep the swing from repeating. In these lessons we will certainly not be attempting to cover all of golf or even one-hundredth of that almost inexhaustible subject. What we will be concerning ourselves with are the facts of golf which have proved themselves to be the true fundamentals—fundamentals that can be checked and not simply left to the imagination or to guesswork. This is all that is really needed.

In the opinion of friends of mine who are out-and-out traditionalists, many of my ideas on the golf swing are quite revolutionary. Some of them are, I believe. As I see it, some measures long esteemed to be of paramount importance in the golf swing are really not important at all. On the other hand, certain other measures that have been considered to be of only secondary importance (or of no importance at all) strike me as being invaluable—to be, in fact, the true fundamentals of the modern golf swing. Another thing. I am an advocate of that kind of teaching which stresses the exact nature and feel of the movements a player makes to achieve the result he wants. If you were teaching a child how to open a door, you wouldn't open the door for him and then describe at length how the door looked when it was open. No, you would teach him how to turn the doorknob so that he could open the door himself. Similarly, in these lessons our method will stress what you do to achieve the result you're after. The actions that cause the result—these are the true fundamentals of golf. For all the personal touches and mannerisms which are part of their individual styles, I have never seen a great player whose method of striking the ball did not include the fundamentals we will emphasize. Otherwise—it is as simple as that—that golfer could not be a great player.

1 The Grip

GOOD GOLF BEGINS WITH A GOOD GRIP. This state-
ment, I realize, packs as much explosive punch as announcing
the startling fact that the battery in baseball is composed
of a pitcher and a catcher. Moreover, for most golfers the
grip is the drabbest part of the swing. There's no glamour
to it. They see it accomplishing nothing active, nothing
decisive. On the other hand, for myself and other serious
golfers there is an undeniable beauty in the way a fine player
sets his hands on the club. Walter Hagen, for instance, had
a beautiful grip, delicate and at the same time powerful. It
always looked to me as if Hagen's hands had been especially
designed to fit on a golf club. Of the younger players today,
Jack Burke gets his hands on the club very handsomely. No
doubt a professional golfer's admiration for an impressive
grip comes from his knowledge that, far from being a static
"still life" sort of thing, the grip is the heartbeat of the action
of the golf swing.

Logically, it has to be. The player's only contact with the
ball is through the clubhead, and his only direct physical
contact with the club is through his hands. In the golf swing,
the power is originated and generated by the movements of
the body. As this power builds up, it is transferred from the

*A golfer's power is originated and generated by the movements
of the body. This power is transferred from the player's body
to his arms and then to his hands. It multiplies itself enormously
with every transfer, like a chain action in physics*

body to the arms, which in turn transfer it through the hands to the clubhead. It multiplies itself enormously with every transfer, like a chain action in physics. Or, to use a more familiar example, think of the children's game of snap-the-whip where the element at the end of the chain (in golf, the clubhead) is going thousands of times faster than the element which originated the velocity. This chain action depends on a proper grip. With a defective grip, a golfer cannot hold the club securely at the top of the backswing—the club will fly out of control every time. And if the club is not controlled by a proper grip, the power a golfer generates with his body never reaches the club through his hands on the downswing, and the clubhead cannot be accelerated to its maximum.

The standard grip is the overlapping grip. It has been for over half a century now, ever since Harry Vardon popularized it both in Great Britain and here in America. Up to now we haven't found a grip that promotes as effective a union between the body and the club. One of these days a better one may come along, but until it does, we've got to stick with this one. In a good grip both hands act as ONE UNIT. They can't if you grip the club almost correctly—which really means partially incorrectly. To cite the most common illustration, a right-handed player (whose left hand naturally is much less powerful than his right) kills any chance for a cooperative union of both hands if his right hand is dominant from the start or if it can assume dominance in the middle of the swing and take the whole swing over. One essential, then, to insure yourself a firm two-handed grip is to get your left hand on the club absolutely correctly. Here's how I would advise you to do it:

WITH THE BACK OF YOUR LEFT HAND FACING THE TARGET (AND THE CLUB IN THE GENERAL POSITION IT WOULD BE IN AT ADDRESS) PLACE THE CLUB IN THE LEFT HAND SO THAT 1) THE SHAFT IS PRESSED UP UNDER THE MUSCULAR PAD AT THE INSIDE HEEL OF THE PALM, AND

2) THE SHAFT ALSO LIES DIRECTLY ACROSS THE TOP JOINT OF THE FOREFINGER. (The accompanying drawing will clarify this for you. I think you will find that whatever subsequent difficulties may arise from the necessarily involved language of instruction will be resolved by the drawings.)

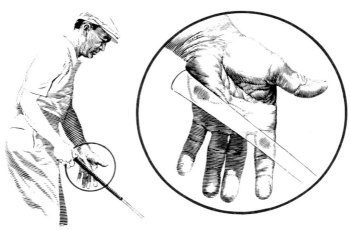

CROOK THE FOREFINGER AROUND THE SHAFT AND YOU WILL DISCOVER THAT YOU CAN LIFT THE CLUB AND MAINTAIN A FAIRLY FIRM GRIP ON IT BY SUPPORTING IT JUST WITH THE MUSCLES OF THAT FINGER AND THE MUSCLES OF THE PAD OF THE PALM.

NOW JUST CLOSE THE LEFT HAND—CLOSE THE
FINGERS BEFORE YOU CLOSE THE THUMB—AND
THE CLUB WILL BE JUST WHERE IT SHOULD BE.

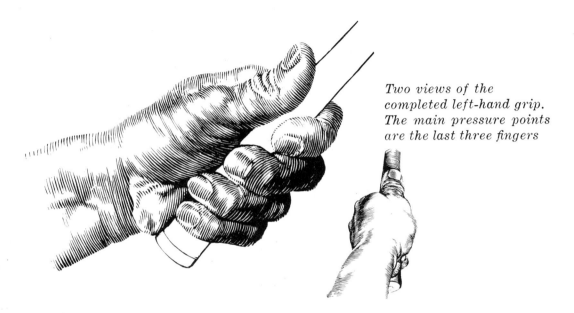

*Two views of the
completed left-hand grip.
The main pressure points
are the last three fingers*

TO GAIN A REAL ACQUAINTANCE WITH THIS
PREPARATORY GUIDE TO CORRECT GRIPPING,
I WOULD SUGGEST PRACTICING IT FIVE OR 10
MINUTES A DAY FOR A WEEK UNTIL IT BEGINS
TO BECOME SECOND NATURE.

When a golfer has completed his left-hand grip, the V
formed by the thumb and forefinger should point to his right
eye. The total pressure of all the fingers should not be any
stronger (and may even be a little less strong) than the pressure exerted by just the forefinger and the palm pad in the
preparatory guiding action. In the completed grip, the main
pressure points are the last three fingers, with the forefinger
and the palm pad adding assisting pressure. The three fingers press up, the pad presses down, and the shaft is locked
in between. Keeping pressure on the shaft with the palm pad

does three things: it strengthens the left arm throughout the swing; at the top of the backswing, the pressure from this pad prevents the club from slipping from the player's grasp; and it acts as a firm reinforcement at impact.

This pressure we are speaking of should be "active," the kind of pressure that makes your hand feel alive and ready for action. Some golfers grab hold of a club so ferociously they look like they're going to twist the grip right off it. There's no need for overdoing the strength of your grip. In fact, there's a positive harm in it: you automatically tighten the cords in the left arm and render it so stiff, so deaf that it will be unable to hear your requests and give you a muscular response when you start your swing. Too tight a grip will also immobilize your wrist. A secure, alive, and comfortable grip is what you want, for, as the weighted clubhead is swung back, your fingers instinctively tighten their grasp on the shaft.

Left-hand grip at top of backswing

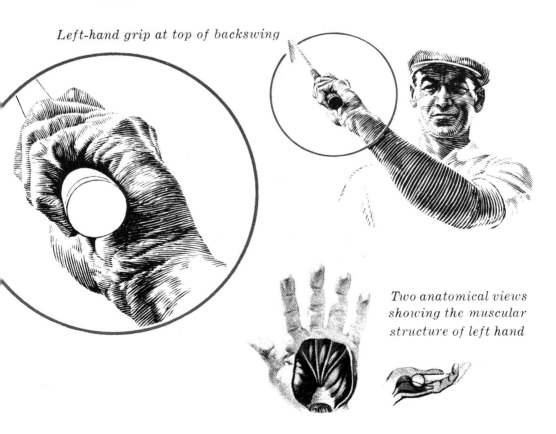

Two anatomical views showing the muscular structure of left hand

This drawing of the completed grip shows the proper positioning of the right hand.

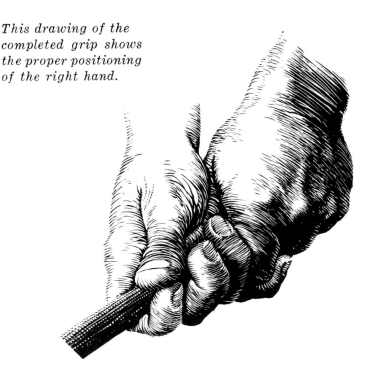

The grip of the right hand, since it is the hand that does the overlapping, is more complicated. If setting up a strong, correct left hand is one half of the job of establishing a one-unit grip, the other half is getting your right hand in a position to perform its share of the work but no more than its equal share. This means, in effect, subduing the natural tendency of the right forefinger and thumb to take charge. If they do, they'll ruin you. The "pincer fingers," the forefinger and thumb, are wonderful for performing countless tasks in daily living such as opening doors and picking up coffee cups, but they are no good at all in helping you to build a good grip and a good swing. The explanation behind this is that the muscles of the right forefinger and thumb connect with the very powerful set of muscles that run along the outside of the right arm and elbow to the right shoulder. If you work the tips of the thumb and forefinger together and apply any considerable amount of pressure, you automatically activate those muscles of the right arm and shoulder—and those are not the muscles you want to use in the golf swing. Using them is what breeds so many golfers who never swing with both hands working together, who lurch back and then lurch into the ball, all right arm and right shoulder and all wrong.

TO OBTAIN THE PROPER GRIP WITH THE RIGHT HAND, HOLD IT SOMEWHAT EXTENDED, WITH THE PALM FACING YOUR TARGET. NOW—YOUR LEFT HAND IS ALREADY CORRECTLY AFFIXED —PLACE THE CLUB IN YOUR RIGHT HAND SO THAT THE SHAFT LIES ACROSS THE TOP JOINT OF THE FOUR FINGERS AND DEFINITELY BELOW THE PALM.

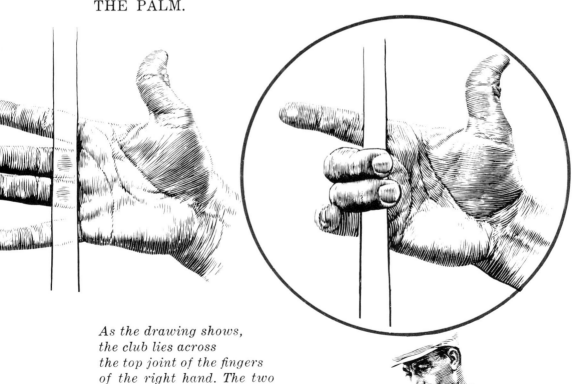

As the drawing shows, the club lies across the top joint of the fingers of the right hand. The two middle fingers supply the major part of the pressure

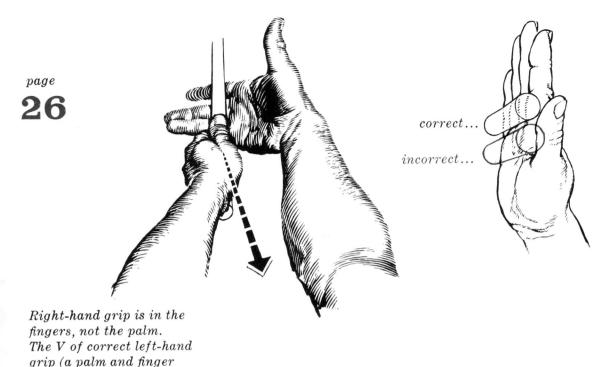

correct...

incorrect...

*Right-hand grip is in the
fingers, not the palm.
The V of correct left-hand
grip (a palm and finger
grip) should point to
golfer's right eye*

THE RIGHT-HAND GRIP IS A FINGER GRIP. THE
TWO FINGERS WHICH SHOULD APPLY MOST OF
THE PRESSURE ARE THE TWO MIDDLE FINGERS.
As we have mentioned, the forefinger shouldn't be allowed
to become too forceful. As for the little finger, it slides up and
over the forefinger of the left hand and locks itself securely
in the groove between the left forefinger and the big finger.
NOW, WITH THE CLUB HELD FIRMLY IN THE FIN-
GERS OF YOUR RIGHT HAND, SIMPLY FOLD YOUR
RIGHT HAND OVER YOUR LEFT THUMB—that is how
I like to think of it. When you have folded the right hand over,
the right thumb should ride down the left side of the shaft,
slightly.

If there is one major consideration to keep uppermost in
your mind about the right hand, it is that the club must be
in the fingers and not in the palm. In order to get a check on
the ball with backspin or to cut the ball up with a nice under-

spin and to do many other things with the ball, the ball must be hit sharp and crisp, and you can achieve this only if the club is in the fingers of the right hand. Furthermore, a proper right-hand grip will enable the player to transmit the greatest amount of speed to the clubhead. Controlled speed is what we want, and you can get this control only from the fingers, not from the right hand itself.

A word more about the little finger of the right hand. While it has been approved practice for quite some time to let the little finger ride sort of piggyback on top of the left forefinger, I would really advise you to hook that little finger in the groove between the forefinger and the big finger. It helps to keep the hands from slipping apart. It also gives me the good feeling that my hands are knitted vigorously together.

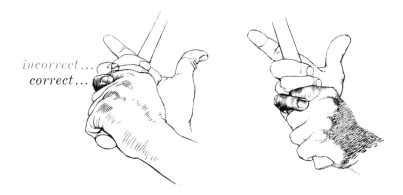

incorrect...
correct...

A word further about the thumb area of the right hand. To promote a right-hand grip that is strong where it should be strong (and which will then more than offset the dangerous tendency to let the tips of thumb and forefinger work like a pincer), I recommend the golfer-reader to cultivate the following habit: School yourself when you are taking your grip so that the thumb and the adjoining part of the hand across the V—the part that is the upper extension of the forefinger— press up against each other tightly, as inseparable as Siamese twins. Keep them pressed together as you begin to affix your grip, and maintain this airtight pressure between them when you fold the right hand over the left thumb. In this connection, I like to feel that the knuckle on the back of my right hand above the forefinger is pressing to the left, toward my target. It rides almost on top of the shaft. I know then that the club has to be in my fingers. Furthermore, when you fold the right hand over the left thumb—and there is a lot left to fold over—the left thumb will fit perfectly in the "cup" formed in the palm of your folded right hand. They fit together like pieces in a jigsaw puzzle.

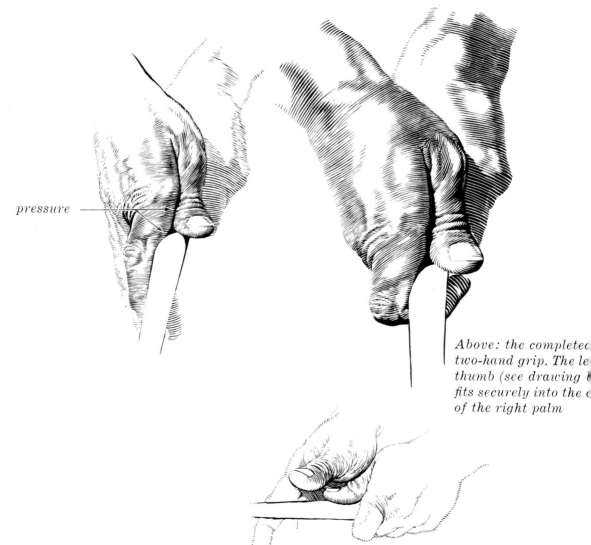

pressure

Above: the completed two-hand grip. The le[ft] thumb (see drawing [below?] fits securely into the c[up] of the right palm

This union of left thumb and right thumb pad strengthens the welding together of the two hands and it serves to add real reinforcement to your grip, particularly at the top of the backswing where poor grips are most likely to deteriorate. When you check your right-hand grip, the V formed by the thumb and forefinger should be pointing right at the button of your chin.

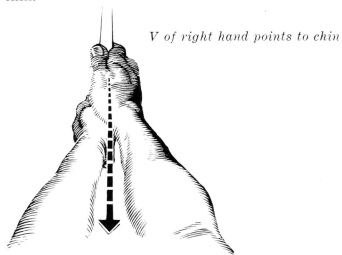

V of right hand points to chin

And a final word about those potential swing-wreckers, the right forefinger and thumb. While the tips of the forefinger and thumb do serve the advanced golfer as his finesse fingers, learning to use them only for touch in striking the ball requires some training. You will develop this talent as you go along. However, at this stage of the game when breaking down bad habits and acquiring correct new habits is our paramount consideration, there is no doubt whatsoever in my mind that the average golfer should forget about this finesse business completely. It can do him so much more harm than good in learning how to use the right hand. In this connection, an extremely beneficial exercise to practice (perhaps five minutes daily for a week) is to grip the club and swing it with the right forefinger and thumb entirely off the shaft. This gives a golfer a wonderful sense of having just one corporate hand on the club. This, of course, is the ideal. When you complete your grip, try to feel that the tips of the forefinger and thumb are hardly on the club and strive instead to build up that opposite feeling (which we described earlier) that the knuckle above the forefinger is pressing toward the thumb and toward the target.

It may seem that we have gone into unwarranted detail about the elements of the correct grip. This is anything but the case. Too often in golf, players mistake the generality for the detail. They think, for example, that overlapping the finger is the detail and so they do not pay sufficient attention to how they do it. Or they confuse an effect (which can be quite superficial) with the action (the real thing) that causes the effect. For instance, a lot of golfers are under the impression that if their two Vs are pointed correctly, their grip must be correct. It may be or may not be. The direction of the Vs is no guarantee, simply a check point. In golf there are certain things you must do quite precisely, where being approximately right is not right enough. The grip is one of these areas where being half right accomplishes nothing. On the other hand, once you start cultivating the right habits, gripping the club correctly comes easily. You'll fall right into it. Furthermore, being painstaking about learning to grip rewards you a thousand times over. Once you have mastered a correct grip—and assuming your stance and posture are also correct—you can practically forget about what the hands will be doing, or what they have to do, during the swing. They will take care of it themselves. The reason for this is that a correct grip brings into play the correct muscles of your arms and body.

I would like to support these points, if I may, with a chunk of autobiography, for if any golfer ever ran the whole gamut of grips, I did. I was born left-handed—that was the normal way for me to do things. I was switched over to doing things right-handed when I was a boy but I started golf as a left-

*Gripping the club with the
right thumb and forefinger
off shaft helps a golfer
to accustom himself to the
feeling of strong, correct
grip in which both hands
work together as one unit*

hander because the first club I ever came into possession of, an old five-iron, was a left-handed stick. I stopped being a left-handed golfer for what might be termed local commercial conditions: the boys in my home town, Fort Worth, used to buy their golf clubs (at a dollar per club) at a five-and-dime store, and there simply never was any left-handed equipment in the barrel where the clubs were stacked. When I changed over to the right side, possibly as a hangover from my left-handed start I first used a cross-hand grip. I experimented next with the interlocking grip, and at length—I must have been about 15 at the time—I finally arrived at the overlapping grip. I was working then in the golf shop at the Glen Garden club, and I copied the grip of Ted Longworth, the pro. I recognized quickly that this was the best of all grips, and once I had persuaded myself of that fact, it took me only a short time to familiarize myself with it.

Over the years since first adopting the overlapping grip, I have made two minor alterations. Right after I came out of the service, I changed from what is called the "long thumb," the left thumb fully extended down the shaft, to a modified "short thumb," contracting my left thumb and pulling it up a half inch. The "long thumb" let the club drop down too far at the top of the backswing, and it was really rough to get my timing right. I made my second alteration in 1946, moving my left hand a good half inch to the left. I was working then to find some way of retaining my power while curbing my occasional tendency to hook. Moving my left hand over so that the thumb was directly down the middle of the shaft was the first step in licking that problem. I regard both of these changes as personal modifications or adjustments. That is, they were beneficial for me and I would advocate them as sound measures for golfers with the same natural swing pattern and hitting action as myself. Let me make it clear, though, that I look upon them only as adjustments and not as fundamentals. The truly fortunate golfer is the player who needs to make the smallest number of adjustments.

The golf grip is bound to function most effectively when the hands and fingers feel thin. Some days they do, some days they don't. Interestingly enough, drinking some ginger ale, because of its effect on the kidneys, seems to prevent the hands from feeling too fat and puffy. If the weather is cold, of course, it always affects your feel. To make sure my hands were warm enough at Carnoustie, I carried a hand-warmer in each pocket. These are Victorian gadgets that work something like a cigarette lighter; the small metal containers (covered with heavy cloth) are filled with a fluid that, once the wick is lit, smolders for about eight hours. These hand-warmers, incidentally, also served to keep the golf balls in my pocket nice and warm. A warm ball, you know, flies farther than a cold one.

In our next lesson, we will take up the modern fundamentals of the stance and posture. But don't go too fast. *For at least a week* PUT IN 30 MINUTES OF DAILY PRACTICE ON THE GRIP. LEARNING THESE NEXT FUNDAMENTALS WILL THEN BE TWICE AS EASY AND TWICE AS VALUABLE. I want to stress again that intelligent application is required to learn the golf swing, but how self-rewarding this application is! The average golfer will finally learn how to put all the elements of the swing together. He will be able to repeat that swing and to hit shots that have the same basic character as a professional's because he will be using the same method a pro does. He may not be as long as a pro or as accurate, but he will be long and straight. And he will be hitting correctly executed golf shots, with real character to them. That is something a lot of people have never experienced, but it is entirely within the average person's power. I cannot emphasize this point too strongly.

Once the average golfer is properly started on the correct

*If his grip is faulty, the
golfer won't have control of
club when he reaches
the top of his backswing*

*If his grip is correct, the
club will be held perfectly
under control at the top
of the player's backswing*

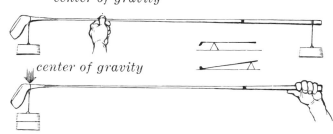

center of gravity

*With fulcrum (hands)
at end of shaft, the center
of gravity is changed
and clubhead feels
much heavier*

center of gravity

method of hitting the golf ball, he will begin to improve and to feel that improvement, and he will gradually find that he is able to hit fine, full shots and to hit the ball high, low, draw it, fade it, play sand shots, recoveries, half shots—ALL THIS WITHOUT CHANGING HIS SWING. The swing itself is what gives you this feel for managing this full variety of golf shots.

As he improves, the average golfer will enjoy the game more and more, for a correct swing will enable him to re-discover golf—in fact, to discover golf for the first time. He will have the necessary equipment, the full "vocabulary" for golf. He's going to see a different game entirely. When he gets on a tee where a 170-yard minimum carry is needed to get across a water hazard, he won't go blank over the ball, as some golfers do, and just pray that somehow he will get it over the water, this being the best he can hope for. No, he'll know he can carry 200 yards of water any old time and he'll honestly be able to think about the more advanced things: how much of the water hazard he should try to cut off, the best position (for a player of his individual length) across the water from which to play his second on the particular hole. The strategy implicit on every good golf hole will appeal to him, not befuddle him. He'll understand the reason why that tree is standing along the left edge of the fairway. He'll see why that trap edges into the opening to the green. He'll see why the fairway narrows where it does. He will not want the greens committee to cut down that tree or close up that trap or push back the rough. He will even object if there is a plan afoot to soften up the rough.

He will, in short, absorb the spirit of the game. When he hits a poor shot and leaves himself with a difficult recovery, he'll respond to the challenge of having to play a difficult shot extra well in order to make up for his error. If there's a small opening to the green, he will respond to that challenge of having to hit a more accurate shot than he usually does or pay the just consequences. He will feel this way about golf because he will know he has an essentially correct, repeating swing and that he can, with moderate concentration, produce the shot that is called for. He will make errors, of course, because he is human, but he will be a golfer and the game will be a source of ever-increasing pleasure for him.

2 Stance and Posture

One of the great fascinations of golf is the instinctive feeling a player gets soon after he has taken the game up that there is an explanation for everything that takes place, that the seeming mystery of how to hit the ball well and hit it well regularly is not mysterious at all, that it is possible to arrive at answers that will be as clear-cut and irrefutable as the solution the master detective unfolds in the last chapter of a mystery novel. All of us, quite like detectives, set off on our own separate paths. We develop a clue here, put it to the test to see if it holds up, develop another lead there, test this lead in turn to see if it will hold up, and so on and on. It is not an easy job. Today's brilliant deduction all too often folds under deeper examination and becomes tomorrow's dead end. And more than that, with no trouble at all you can get off on the wrong track, increase your error by studiously taking the wrong turn at another crucial fork in the road, and before you know it you are lost in a labyrinth of your own making. Perhaps the only true mystery to golf is the essential magnetism the game possesses which makes so many of us, regardless of discouragement, never quite turn in our trench coats and magnifying glasses and stop our search for the answers.

Golf also seems to bring out the scientist in a person. He soon discovers that unless he goes about observing and testing with an orderly method, he is simply complicating his problems. In this general connection, I found out that it helps me immensely to bring along a notebook and pencil to the practice tee and to write down after each session just what it was I had been working on, exactly how it was coming, and precisely where it was that I should resume my testing the next time I went out to practice. I will probably keep on studying golf all my life, but I honestly feel that I have now acquired a sound understanding of the game that will be of real value to all golfers. How I wish I had known what I know today when I was a youngster just starting out!

As I said in the first lesson, no one can play good golf unless he has a correct, powerful, repeating swing. A man or woman of average coordination can build such a swing if he or she goes about it sensibly. It really boils down to learning and practicing a few fundamentals until performing them becomes almost as instinctive as walking. There are not as many things to learn as you might think, for the swing we are teaching has been stripped down to the authentic essentials. The only "technical" thing about this swing is the explanation. There is a definite purpose behind every movement.

The first of these inclusive fundamentals is, of course, the grip, which we already have discussed. The second is the stance and the posture. Many golfers make the sizable error of thinking of the stance as that preparatory part of the swing in which the player merely lines himself up on the target he's shooting at. While one of the purposes of the stance certainly is to set up the direction of the shot, it also has quite a number of other functions that are much more important. Power and control must be combined in a good golf swing, and the stance is that step in which a golfer sets himself up so that 1) his body will be in balance

*The proper stance and
posture enable a golfer to be
perfectly balanced and
poised throughout the
swing. Only then will his
legs, arms, and body
be able to carry out
their interrelated
assignments correctly*

throughout the swing, 2) his muscles are ready to perform fluidly and, 3) as a logical result, all the energy he pours into his swing will be channeled to produce maximum control and power. When you see a fine player making little individual movements of his feet or his knees or his shoulders as he settles into his stance, do not mistake these for empty gestures of nervousness. And they're not movements, either, that precede his arriving at a static, fixed position. What he's actually trying to do is to *feel* that everything he will be calling on in his swing is in balance and poised for action.

When a golfer steps up to his ball to play a shot—mind you, he already has his grip on the club and from the moment he took the club from his bag he should be getting the feel of the weight—he first aligns the face of his club with his target. Then, aligning himself with the face of the club, he shuffles into position for the upcoming shot. The adjustment of the feet, the legs, the body, the arms and hands—all these are done simultaneously, interdependently. However, for the purposes of instruction, we will take them up one at a time, and we will start with the feet.

To begin with, how far apart should the feet be? The soundest rule, since it applies for people of nearly all builds, is that THE FEET SHOULD BE SET APART THE WIDTH OF THE SHOULDERS WHEN YOU ARE PLAYING A STANDARD FIVE-IRON SHOT. THEY ARE SET SOMEWHAT CLOSER TOGETHER WHEN YOU PLAY THE MORE LOFTED CLUBS, SOMEWHAT WIDER THAN THE WIDTH OF THE SHOULDERS WHEN YOU PLAY THE LONG IRONS AND THE WOODS. Spreading the feet too far apart is somewhat self-defeating. By over-extending your legs, you may lock them at joints that must remain supple. I do want to bring out, however, that most golfers take too narrow a stance. I advocate a stance that is fairly wide because it gives you a firmer foundation for traction and balance, and it permits the shoulders to be unbunched and to operate more freely than a narrow stance does.

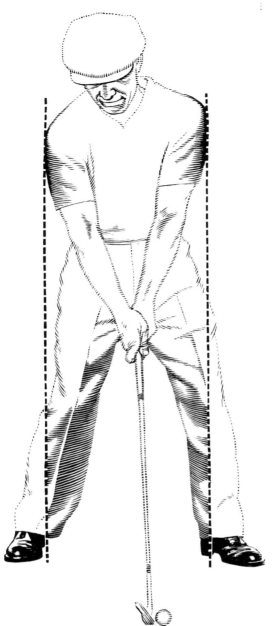

The feet should be set apart the width of the shoulders when the golfer prepares to play a standard five-iron shot

Some tournament-caliber golfers, as you may have noticed, choose to stand with the toes of both feet pointed out. It has always struck me that these players succeed in spite of the placement of their feet, for I have been convinced since my early days in golf that THERE IS ONE CORRECT BASIC STANCE: THE RIGHT FOOT

IS AT A RIGHT ANGLE TO THE LINE OF FLIGHT
AND THE LEFT FOOT IS TURNED OUT A
QUARTER OF A TURN TO THE LEFT.

The term *a quarter of a turn* may be confusing, and I had better explain that what I have in mind is that placing your left foot so that the toe would be pointing right at the target would amount to a full 90-degree turn from a position perpendicular to the line of flight. In other words, a quarter of a turn signifies a quarter of that 90-degree angle, or about 22 degrees to the left of perpendicular.

When a player employs this stance, his body will be in a much better position when the club is coming into the ball on the downswing to go in the direction in which his left foot is going. As a matter of fact, you can tell just from looking at a good golfer's stance exactly where he is aiming

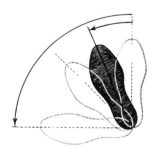

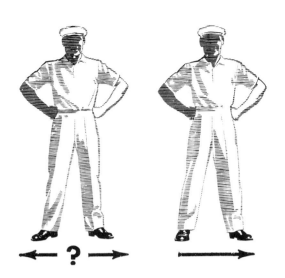

to hit his shot. Most pros even tend to list their bodies a little toward the target at address. On the other hand, a golfer who stands with both feet turned out makes you wonder to yourself, "Is this fellow going to hit the ball right-handed or left-handed?" His stance gives you no clue in which direction he's going.

Obeying the basic stance accomplishes several very important things, the full value of which will become clearer and clearer as the lessons progress. FIRST, IT MAKES IT APPRECIABLY EASIER FOR THE GOLFER, AS HE GOES INTO HIS BACKSWING, TO FEEL AND CONTROL THE MUSCLES THAT SHOULD INITIATE THE SWING. SECOND, THE CORRECT STANCE ACTS AS A PERFECT AUTOMATIC GOVERNOR ON THE AMOUNT OF HIP TURN THE GOLFER CAN TAKE (AND SHOULD TAKE) ON THE BACKSWING. It allows the hips to be rotated as far around as is advisable, but it prevents them from being rotated too far around. Now, if the player stands with his left foot squared (or perpendicular) and not turned out as it should be, when the hips are turned—since they start at a point nearer to the right and rear—they will turn well beyond the point of maximum desirable rotation. If a player's right foot is turned out instead of squared, this also allows his hips to turn further around than is advisable.

Here are some check points to use when you are practicing your hip turn: When you start from the correct basic stance and complete a full hip turn, your belt buckle should point toward the toe of your squared right foot. However, when you start from the faulty stances we've described above, your hip turn will carry you well past this check point and your belt buckle will be pointing in almost the exact opposite direction from your target.

Third, the stance also affects the downswing, a very great deal. By standing with his right foot pointed out, for example, a player definitely makes it much harder for himself to bring the club swiftly and smoothly into the ball and through it. He has obstructed his own passage forward. He has to go on a detour out and around his right hip to get past it. He also makes things hard for himself in a different way if he stands with his left foot squared and not turned out that vital quarter of a turn. I know that if I stand with my left foot squared, my left leg and my whole body feel uncomfortably restricted when I'm hitting through the ball. Instead of everything moving cohesively and freely toward my target, everything is grinding under strain. IF YOUR LEFT FOOT IS CORRECTLY POSITIONED, ON THE OTHER HAND, YOU CAN GO THROUGH THE BALL WITH EVERYTHING YOU'VE GOT. YOU CAN RELEASE THE WHOLE WORKS. THERE ISN'T AN OUNCE OF ENERGY THAT ISN'T IMPARTED TO THE BALL.

The fact that an apparently insignificant detail like the position of the left foot can affect your entire swing for better or for worse is an intrinsic part of golf. The explanation is, of course, anatomical—not that we will pursue this at all deeply. In any event, certain muscles

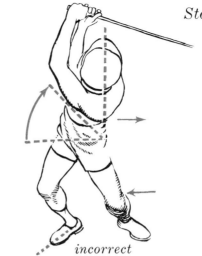

incorrect

The incorrect positioning of the right foot can lead to many serious errors, including dipping the left knee, swaying the right leg out to the right, turning the hips excessively, and making a forced, incorrect shoulder turn as left arm breaks

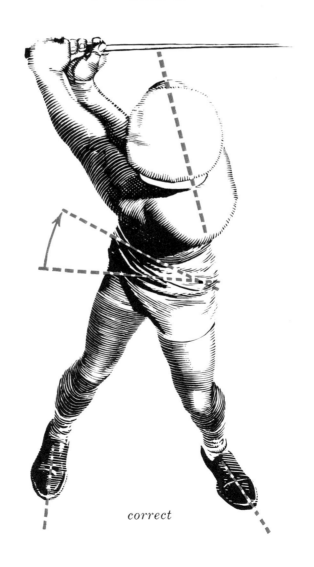

correct

of the body connect with certain other muscles. When you use one muscle in a certain chain, you also activate the others that are connected with it. There are some sets of muscles that should be active in the golf swing, and there are some other sets of muscles that have no real business in the swing. For example, when a golfer overturns his hips going back, then, since he cannot move forward by the proper means—using the hips themselves—he has to call on incorrect sources of power, like his right shoulder, to get some force into his shot. When he brings these incorrect forces into his swing, his coordination breaks down, for by using wrong muscles he necessarily curtails the correct functioning of the correct muscles. That is why it is so important to develop the right habits, proper muscle memory. The way the parts of the body function in the golf swing is, in fact, not unlike a Western movie with heroes and villains: if you set it up so that the good guys take over, the bad guys can't.

Turning now to the arms. During the swing, one of the two arms is always straight—that is, fully extended. There's a very good reason for this. IN ORDER FOR THE CLUB TO TRAVEL ITS MAXIMUM ARC, ONE ARM MUST BE EXTENDED AT ALL TIMES. If a player breaks his left elbow on the backswing or breaks his right elbow on the follow-through, he shortens his arc appreciably. And if he swings with a shorter arc, he gives himself a shorter distance in which he can accelerate the speed with which his club is traveling. (The greater the speed of the club, of course, the greater the distance he will hit the ball.) It's like accelerating an automobile. If you accelerate an automobile over a distance of, say, two blocks, can you get it up to anywhere like the speed you'd obtain if you accelerated it for a distance of five blocks? Moreover, if one of the player's two arms is always extended, his arc will be uniform. This gives him a far better chance of building a repeating swing than a player who bends his arms a little differently on each swing and whose coordination is bound to vary as his arc varies.

The left arm, straight at address, remains straight throughout the backswing while the right folds in at the elbow. On the downswing, the left continues to be fully extended and the right gradually straightens out. A foot or so past the ball, the point in the swing when the clubhead is traveling at its peak speed, both arms are fully extended for the one and only time during the swing. After this point is reached, the left arm folds in at the elbow and the right remains straight to the end of the follow-through. (This is sort of the reverse of the backswing, when the right arm folds in and the left remains straight.) All during the swing, until it begins to fold at that point beyond impact, the left arm ideally should operate as if it were an extension of the shaft. Naturally, there must be some suppleness, some break in your left wrist. After all, it is a hinge. In general, then, though the left arm should be straight, this doesn't mean that it should be locked at the wrist or elbow or be any place as stiff as the arm of a robot. No, this is a very pleasant game, and unnatural straining isn't at all necessary, or desirable.

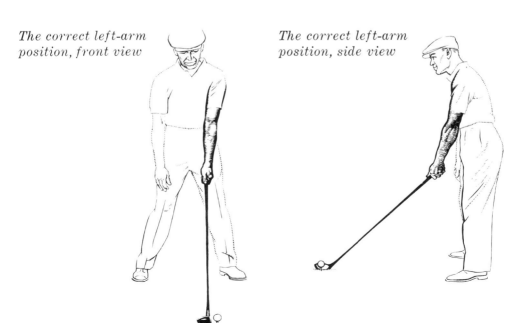

The correct left-arm position, front view

The correct left-arm position, side view

In the golf swing, the arms, in effect, act as the connection between the club and the body. The closer you keep your two arms together, the better they will operate as one unit, and when they operate as one unit, they tend to pull all of the elements of the swing together.

The upper part of the arms should be pressed very tightly against the sides of the chest. In my own case, I consciously work to build up so strong an adhesion between the upper arms and the chest that a person would have to exert a really terrific amount of force to wedge them apart. THE ELBOWS SHOULD BE TUCKED IN, NOT STUCK OUT FROM THE BODY. AT ADDRESS, THE LEFT ELBOW SHOULD POINT DIRECTLY AT THE LEFT HIPBONE AND THE RIGHT ELBOW SHOULD POINT DIRECTLY AT THE RIGHT HIPBONE. FURTHERMORE, THERE SHOULD BE A SENSE OF FIXED JOINTNESS BETWEEN THE TWO FOREARMS AND THE WRISTS, AND IT SHOULD BE MAINTAINED THROUGHOUT THE SWING.

A word of emphasis about the elbows. You want to press them as closely together as you can. When you do this (and the elbows are pointing properly to the hipbones) you will notice that the "pocket" of each elbow—the small depression on the inside of the joint—will lie in the center of the arm, at the midway point. The pockets will be facing toward the sky, as they should, not toward each other. It's a good check. In this position of address, though the left arm hangs relatively straight, the right arm should be broken a little at the elbow as the elbow points in. On the backswing this right elbow must not fly out, and only if it is correctly positioned at address will it be able to fold in close to the body. During the first half of the backswing, the right elbow should move hardly at all. It mustn't slide out laterally or slip back along the right side. As it folds close to the body, the elbow should always be pointing toward the ground. It helps, you will find, if the upper part of the right arm adheres as closely as possible to the side of the chest.

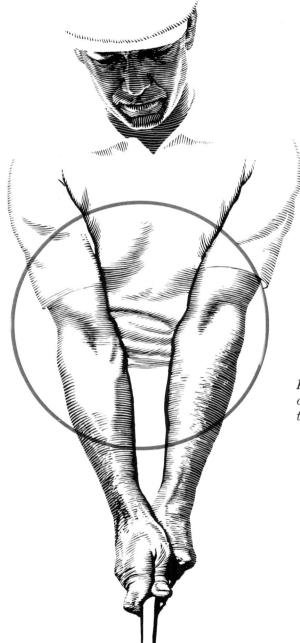

Keep the elbows and arms as close together as possible throughout the entire swing

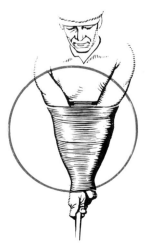

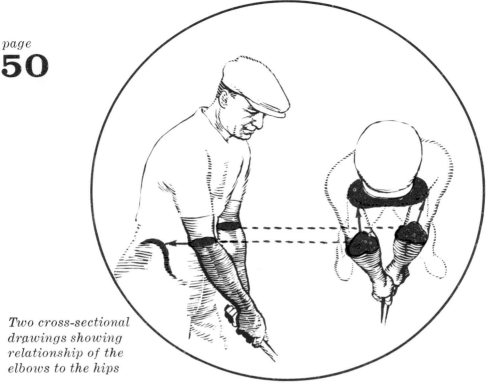

Two cross-sectional drawings showing relationship of the elbows to the hips

When your arms are set right at address, it makes it immeasurably easier to get the proper function out of the arms. With practice, they will act the same way on swing after swing, with no variation, repeating the same action almost like a machine. As your arms become schooled, you will get the feeling that the arms and the club form one firm unit—sort of as if the two arms were equal sides of a triangle, with the club emerging like the spire of a steeple at the peak point where the arms join. As you practice, your arms will recognize with increasing certainness when they are on the right track as they swing back and then forward. "This swing," you will feel more and more surely, "is bound to go away from the ball and come back through the ball very nearly the same way every time." And it will.

Now, before we go into the final phase of stance and posture—how a golfer's legs and his body in general should be flexed as he positions himself over the ball—is perhaps

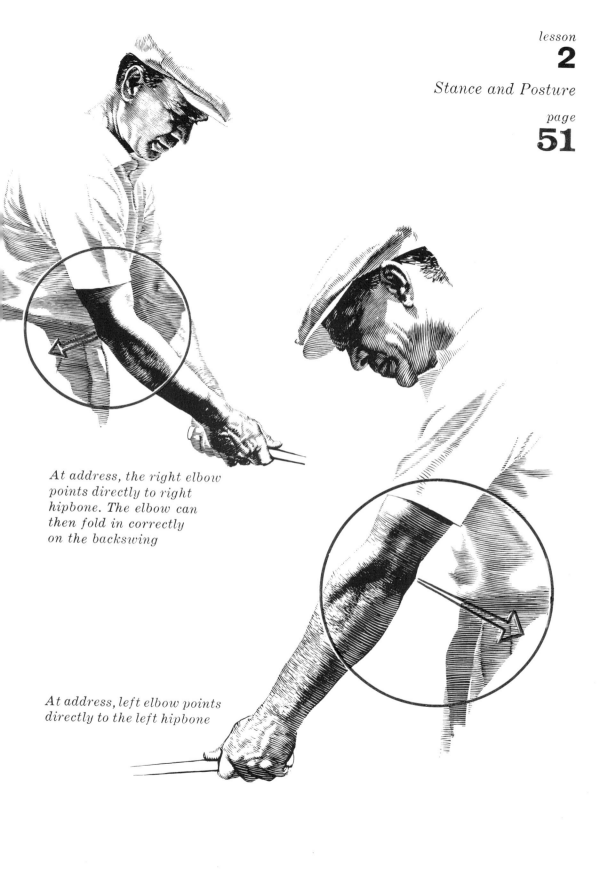

At address, the right elbow
points directly to right
hipbone. The elbow can
then fold in correctly
on the backswing

At address, left elbow points
directly to the left hipbone

the right time and place to interject a brief comment on that greatly overworked and abused word *relaxation*. I would guess that it is harder to achieve proper relaxation in golf than in any other sport. Simply being in motion helps an athlete tremendously to relax. The average golfer's understandable anxiety about whether or not he's going to be able to perform his swing correctly from his next static start is the chief reason he worries his way around the golf course.

There are several ways, all of them connected with understanding what the swing is really about, through which a golfer can help himself to lick this problem. Right off the reel, it will help him if he realizes that *pure* relaxation is something he can't attain and shouldn't want to. There is nothing wrong with a person if he feels a bit keyed up when he goes out to play golf. He should. It is natural. He's going to be doing something that takes some concentration and effort, so he shouldn't expect to feel as free from tension as if he were loafing at home in the evening watching a TV show. No topnotch competitive golfer I have known was, or is, totally relaxed. Each of them feels the pressure of tournament play. Being of different temperaments, they feel it somewhat differently and they absorb it, expressing it or not expressing it, in their individual ways, depending on whether they are Jones or Nelson or Demaret or Middlecoff or Snead or Sarazen or Armour.

There is, however, another type of relaxation—you might call it active relaxation as distinct from passive relaxation. Regardless of how nervously taxed a player may be under the strain of competition, all fine competitive golfers, as they prepare to play a shot and actually play it, manage to be actively relaxed, to be neither limp nor tense but to have live tension in the parts of the body that will be doing the work. They tune up the muscles they will be using, the way a musician tunes up his instrument. The fact that

When he assumes the "semi-sitting position," the upper part of player's trunk remains relatively erect as he bends at the knees. The knees point in

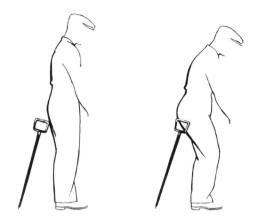

*The sit-down motion is like lowering yourself
(about two inches) onto a spectator-sports-stick*

*Numerous average golfers
fail to realize that an
incorrect stance and faulty
posture greatly affect
the success of the entire
swing. The golfer is off
balance from the start if he
keeps his legs stiff, or lets
his knees buckle, or
crouches his shoulders
way over the ball*

there is something to do, rather than something not to do, is what is so helpful.

The average player, no different from the tournament player, can learn to prepare himself for his shot by positioning himself so that his muscular system is all set to work correctly. ABOVE ALL, HIS KNEES MUST BE PROPERLY FLEXED. THE LEGS MUST BE SUPPLE BUT AT THE SAME TIME THEY MUST HAVE THIS LIVE TENSION. The rest of the body will pick up this athletic temper from the legs. When his knees are flexed as they should be, a player can move his hips and shoulders with a real sense of ease. All the movements, in fact, become easier and more integrated. This is why you hear fine golfers so often remark that the days they play their best golf are invariably those days when their legs are really ready and eager for action.

Assuming the proper posture as he addresses the ball is a purposeful movement in which a player lowers his body from its normal erect position into a sturdier and more balanced position for executing the golf swing. Do not use your hips as you bend your knees. YOU SHOULD BEND YOUR KNEES FROM THE THIGHS DOWN. AS YOUR KNEES BEND, THE UPPER PART OF THE TRUNK REMAINS NORMALLY ERECT, JUST AS IT DOES WHEN YOU SIT DOWN IN A CHAIR. IN GOLF, THE SIT-DOWN MOTION IS MORE LIKE LOWERING YOURSELF ONTO A SPECTATOR-SPORTS-STICK. THINK OF THE SEAT OF THE STICK AS BEING ABOUT TWO INCHES OR SO BELOW YOUR BUTTOCKS. In this semi-sitting position, your body should feel in balance both laterally and back-to-front. You should feel a sense of heaviness in your buttocks. There should be more tension in your legs from the knees down — the lower part of your legs should feel very springy and strong, loaded with elastic energy. Your weight should be a bit more on the heels than on the balls of your feet, so that, if you wanted to, you would be able to lift your toes inside your shoes. The back, let me repeat, remains as naturally erect as it is when you're walking down a fairway. Do not crouch the shoulders over the ball. You bend your head down only by bending your neck, not your back or shoulders.

When you practice this semi-sitting position, have a golf club in your hands and go about it exactly as if you were getting ready to play a shot. When you are standing erect before the ball, you will find that, with your arms normally extended, the head of the club will be raised about four inches above the ball. As you lower yourself into the semi-sitting position — your upper trunk should feel like it's an elevator dropping down a floor — the clubhead descends as your trunk descends. When you have completed the semi-squat, the clubhead should be an inch or two above the ball. Then, with a little motion, the hands set the clubhead behind the ball.

A word further about the knees. During the golf swing, the knees work "toward each other." Since they do, let's start them that way to begin with, each knee pointing in. In my opinion, this is a very valuable short cut, for then you have to move the knees only a very small amount as you swing, and you can concentrate your attention on other movements.

The right knee should be broken a shade more in to the left, if anything, than the left knee is to the right. If the right knee is pointed in, then it's "in business" all the time. It helps brace the right leg on the backswing, and the right leg must be sturdily braced to prevent the golfer from swaying his body laterally to the right as he swings the club back. For another thing, the right knee will then be in the correct position for the downswing when the power of the right hip and leg is released toward the target. If the golfer's right knee is pointed straight ahead or out to begin with, he can bring it in with a separate action on the downswing, of course, but he is making the knee do double work, and there's no sense in that. As for the left knee, having it pointed in just a bit at address is the best insurance in the world for developing proper left-leg action on both the backswing and downswing.

To sum things up generally, then, when you have a correct stance and correct posture, then and only then will your legs, arms and body be properly balanced and positioned to carry out their assignments during the swing. Then and only then will you be able to feel live tension in those arm and leg muscles which must function actively during the swing. NOTE THIS WELL: THE MUSCLES TO WORK WITH ARE THE "INSIDE MUSCLES"— THE MUSCLES THAT STRETCH ALONG THE INSIDE OF THE LEGS AND THIGHS, THE MUSCLES ALONG THE INSIDE OF THE ARMS.

In looking back over this chapter, I can appreciate that it may make acquiring a sound, dependable golf swing seem a slow and painstaking proposition. That isn't exactly true. You can learn these essential positions and movements a lot quicker than you think, provided you get started right. At the same time, some patience is required. You simply cannot bypass the fundamentals in golf any more than you can sit down at the piano without a lesson and rip off the score of *My Fair Lady*. Learning the grip and stance and posture clearly and well is, in a way, like having to practice the scales when you're taking up the piano. In fact, the more I think about it, the best way to learn golf is a great deal like learning to play the piano: you practice a few things daily, you arrive at a solid foundation, and then you go on to practice a few more advanced things daily, continually increasing your skill.

Practice at home can be made more pleasant—and at least as profitable—if you do it along with a fellow golfer, your wife or son or daughter or golfing friend. Then each

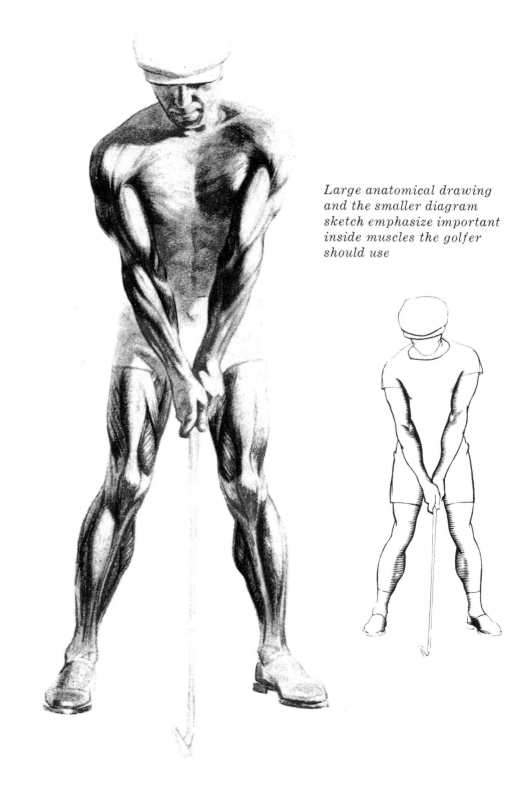

*Large anatomical drawing
and the smaller diagram
sketch emphasize important
inside muscles the golfer
should use*

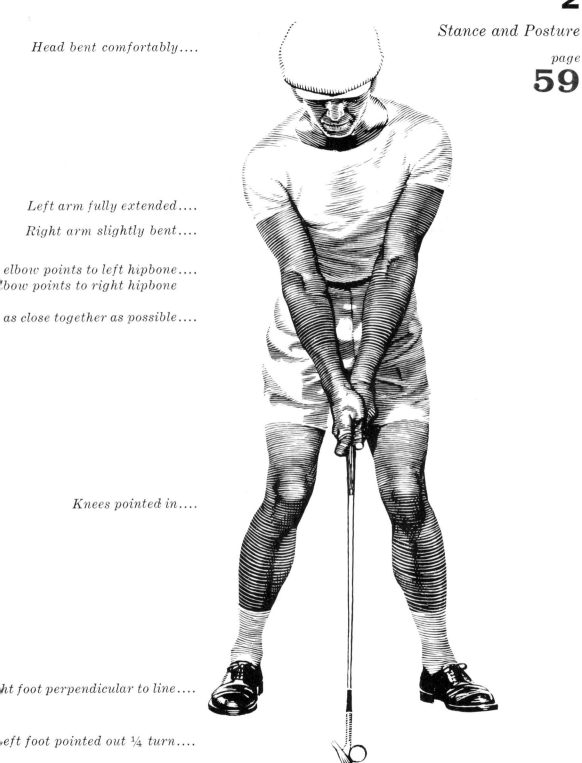

Head bent comfortably....

Left arm fully extended....
Right arm slightly bent....

elbow points to left hipbone....
bow points to right hipbone

as close together as possible....

Knees pointed in....

ht foot perpendicular to line....

eft foot pointed out ¼ turn....

of you can take turns checking how well the other is doing and helping him to correct his errors. Teaching, you know, isn't the worst way to get things straight yourself. If, however, you are a person who prefers to practice things by yourself, let me recommend using a full-length mirror as the best means of checking your moves.

However you choose to practice, bear in mind that the end objective is to build a sound swing, not a swing with only superficial good looks. While I do not claim that I have a model swing or a perfect swing, I do think I know the ingredients that make one. If you learn and apply the precepts these lessons teach, this does not mean that your swing will necessarily be, minute action for minute action, a literal duplicate of mine. Like any individual, my way of executing a fundamental is bound to be somewhat different from what is natural execution for a player whose build or muscular arrangement is different from mine. The big idea, as goes without the saying, is for you to execute the fundamentals properly so that you will have a swing that functions properly. When all is said and done, style is function and function is style. That is why there is a basic resemblance among all fine golfers. Despite their personal mannerisms, in major ways they all do the same things. It may just happen that the "style" you evolve will instantly recall Harry Cooper or Mac Smith to your golfing friends, and that wouldn't be such a bad thing at all.

3 The First Part of the Swing

Some persons who have made golf their career devote the major portion of their working hours to teaching the game. In contrast to the "home pro," other members of my profession are, first and foremost, tournament golfers who follow the circuit. There are a few professionals (but not many) who combine serious teaching and serious competitive golf but, for the most part, keeping himself tuned up for tournament golf takes all of a man's time nowadays because the competition is much keener. Today you have to be a specialist in golf.

In any event, that has been true in my case. Preparing myself for tournaments and participating in them consumed practically all my time and energies. Far from leaving me with extra hours for teaching, it left me only with the regret that the days were not longer so that I could spend more time practicing and preparing.

I have often wondered whether, if the demands of being a tournament golfer had not been so all-encompassing, I would have been a first-class teacher of golf. I really don't know the answer. Certainly I didn't and don't have the ideal temperament for teaching, not compared to such natural teachers as Henry Picard, Claude Harmon and Al

Watrous (who were champions when they were playing tournaments). However, I think I was a pretty fair teacher, providing the pupil was seriously interested in improving his game. Quite early in my career when I was serving as the professional at the Century Country Club in Purchase, N. Y., I did a great deal of teaching. It strikes me now that my general approach to teaching was on the very right path: don't simply tell a player what he's doing wrong—that's not much help. You must explain to him what he ought to be doing, why it is correct, and the result it produces—and work like blazes to get it across so that he really understands what you are talking about.

Generally speaking, a teacher is no better than his pupil's ability to work and to learn. There was a young businessman at my club, Fred Ehrman, who had this ability to learn, and we did a very satisfying job together. He was a 90-shooter in April. Five months later he was playing in the 70s and won the club championship. It was no fluke. The next season, although he was beaten in the final of the club championship by Carl Loeb Jr., his game kept on improving. This took place back in 1938 and 1939. While it is undeniable that the more you know about golf the more you can keep on learning, almost indefinitely, I believe that by 1939 I knew quite well what were the true fundamentals of the golf swing. My knowledge in those days, though, was less integrated than it later became. While I sensed quite clearly the things that were important, I would have had a much harder time in 1939 explaining the reasons why they were. By 1946 I think I truly understood the dynamics of the golf swing.

Beginning in 1946, moreover, I was able to win some of the big championships, and being able to win was the proof I needed that what I felt was correct was indeed correct. It worked. It stood up to the test it was designed to meet. Frequently, you know, what looks like a fairly good golf swing falls apart in competition. Sometimes this is due to the

If the golfer executes his backswing correctly, at the top of his backswing his legs, hips, shoulders, arms and hands will be properly poised and interrelated to move with power and coordination into that climactic part of the golf swing, the downswing

player's temperament—not everyone is built for tournament golf. Much more often, though, the harsh light of competition reveals that a swing is only superficially correct and cannot be schooled for competition because it isn't really correct. It can't stand up day after day. A correct swing will. In fact, the greater the pressure you put on it, the better your swing should function, if it is honestly sound. I feel confident that what I tell you about the true fundamentals is right because the crucible of competition, in which those fundamentals were put to the test, proved to me they were right.

It should be added, of course, that every golfer, no matter how sound his game, must expect to experience some ups and downs. Being a human being, he cannot always be at the peak of his game. He will win his share of tournaments, but there are bound to be occasions when he cannot keep pace with some of his wonderfully talented colleagues who that week happen to be at the peak of *their* games.

The fundamentals of golf, as I see it, fall into four natural groupings: those that relate 1) to the grip, 2) to the stance and posture, 3) to the first part of the swing (from address to the top of the backswing) and 4) to the second part of the swing (from the start of the downswing to the finish of the follow-through). In this chapter we will be discussing the first part of the swing. This phase of the swing requires some instinct, a sense of organization, some thought and a fair control of muscular action. It is, however, much less involved than this makes it appear. Learning the backswing actually consists of getting a few movements clear in your mind and then learning to execute them. This is where the golf shot begins to be played.

The first point about the backswing (and the swing in general) I want to emphasize is this: if his body, legs and arms are properly positioned and poised to begin with, any golfer with average physical equipment can learn to execute the proper movements. This is why you must build on a correct grip and stance, for the golf swing is an accumulative thing. All the actions are linked together.

For instance, when your grip is correct you will have the proper live tension in the muscles which run along the inside of the arms all the way to the armpit. These are the arm muscles you want to work with—they tie in with the muscles of the body that should be used in the golf swing. Coordinated movement results. Same thing with the legs. The inside muscles which stretch from the ankle to the thigh are the right ones for golf. When a player uses them—to cite just one illustration—his left knee is bound to break in correctly to the right on the backswing. It won't shoot out straight ahead and, as it buckles, cause his whole body to buckle over with it. Just as one faulty movement leads to others, each correct movement makes it that much easier to execute other moves correctly. With practice, these movements will all blend harmoniously together and fuse into one smooth over-all movement. A bad swing is tiring drudgery. A good swing is a physical pleasure.

The bridge between the address and the actual start of the backswing is "the waggle." As a golfer looks at his objective and figures out the kind of shot he's going to play, his instinct takes over: he waggles the club back and forth. Possibly because the word *waggle* suggests that any aimless kind of oscillation fills the bill, many golfers have the mistaken idea that it doesn't really matter how you waggle the club. To put it another way, they think the only purpose in waggling is to loosen yourself up so that you won't be tense or rigid. There's a great deal more to the waggle than that. It is an extremely important part of shotmaking. Far from being just a lot of minute details, it is a sort of miniature practice swing, an abbreviated "dry run" for the shot coming up. As the golfer takes the club back on the waggle, he accustoms himself to the path the club will be taking on his actual backswing. As he waggles the club forward, he adjusts himself so that the face of the clubhead will be coming into the ball square and on the line.

During the waggle, as he previews his shot and attempts to telegraph his mental picture from his brain to his muscles, the golfer makes the little adjustments necessary to be perfectly in balance for hitting that particular shot from that particular lie. As he waggles, he tunes himself up and tones himself up for his swing. The shoulders do not turn during the waggle. The feet make only small adjusting movements. The hands and arms move. As they waggle the club, the hands and arms pass their rhythm, their tempo of coordination, on to the legs and feet. The trunk of the body and the shoulders pick up this beat, smoothly, from the arms and the legs. The whole body, in effect, becomes synchronized to the rhythm in which the various parts will be working cohesively together during the swing.

If you take full advantage of the opportunity the waggle affords, you can practically rehearse the swing you'll be using. I know that I have sometimes concentrated so hard on the shot I was going to hit that I honestly felt the shot could not fail to come off exactly as I intended. On those occasions I had the definite sensation that I had really hit the shot before I even started my club back.

In the waggle, the left hand is the controlling hand. The right works along with the left. EACH TIME YOU WAGGLE THE CLUB BACK, THE RIGHT ELBOW SHOULD HIT THE FRONT PART OF YOUR RIGHT HIP, JUST ABOUT WHERE YOUR WATCH POCKET IS. WHEN THIS TAKES PLACE, THE LEFT ELBOW, AS IT MUST, COMES OUT SLIGHTLY, THE LOWER PART OF THE ARM FROM THE ELBOW DOWN ROTATES A LITTLE, AND THE LEFT HAND MOVES THREE INCHES OR SO PAST THE BALL TOWARD THE TARGET. AS THE HANDS MOVE BACK TO THE BALL ON THE FORWARD WAGGLE, THE LEFT HAND

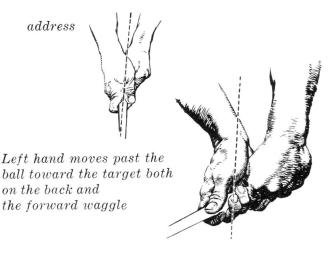

address

Left hand moves past the ball toward the target both on the back and the forward waggle

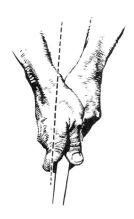

back waggle   *forward waggle*

ALSO MOVES AN INCH OR TWO PAST THE BALL TOWARD THE TARGET. During the waggle, the upper part of the arms remain rooted against the sides of the chest. As we stated earlier, there should be no turning of the shoulders.

When a good golfer is going through his waggle, to the uninitiated eye it sometimes looks as if he were simply getting the fidgets out of his system or finding a surer foothold with his spikes. He is, as I have described, doing something far more purposeful than that. He's adjusting to the shot, establishing his coordination in the process. He is, in effect, conducting an instinctive roll call of the parts of the body he will be using, alerting them and refreshing their memory of the movements they'll be making during the swing.

The rhythm of the waggle varies with each shot you play. DON'T GROOVE YOUR WAGGLE. IT TAKES INSTINCT TO PLAN AND PLAY A GOLF SHOT, AND YOUR PREPARATIONS FOR EACH SHOT MUST BE DONE INSTINCTIVELY. Let's say, for example, that you're 130 yards out from a semiplateau green. You've decided that you want to get the ball well up in the air in

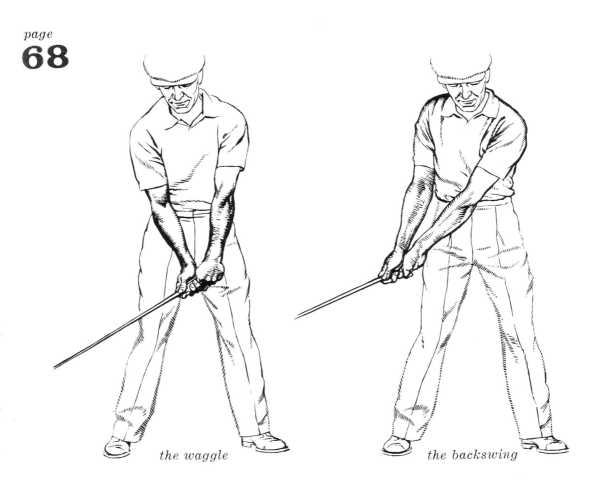

the waggle *the backswing*

During the waggle the shoulders do not turn.
On the actual swing they do. The hands, arms and the shoulders
start to move almost simultaneously on the backswing

a steep trajectory, and that you'll be playing a seven-iron. You want to strike the shot firmly, as goes without saying, but you want to hit a soft, feathery kind of shot that will float down onto the green. Well, you'll waggle somewhat slowly, somewhat softly. This is the tempo you will also be using on the stroke, of course. Say, on the other hand, that you've got to bang a drive low into the wind on a hole where it's important to be out a good distance from the tee to get home in two. For this shot, you'll move the club back and forth with much more briskness, more conviction, more speed. And you'll swing that way. The waggle, in other words, fits the shot.

The waggle gives the golfer a running start. It blends right into the swing. For all general points and purposes, the backswing is simply an extension of the way the golfer takes the club back on the waggle. The club follows that same path and it is swung back at the speed the waggle has regulated. There is, however, one significant difference between the waggle and the backswing which must be made crystal-clear. DURING THE WAGGLE, THE SHOULDERS DO NOT TURN. ON THE ACTUAL SWING, THEY DO, RIGHT FROM THE BEGINNING OF THE BACKSWING. THE BACKSWING IS, IN FACT, INITIATED BY THE ALMOST SIMULTANEOUS MOVEMENT OF THE HANDS, ARMS AND SHOULDERS. Introducing the shoulders does not alter the pattern you set up in the waggle. By turning your shoulders on your actual backswing, you simply increase the arc of your waggle.

Throughout these lessons we have placed special emphasis on the fact that the golf swing is, in principle, a continuous chain of actions. Like the component parts of the engine of an automobile, the component parts of the swing fuse together and work together in a purposeful sequence. As each component performs its part of the operation, it sets up the proper operation of the other components with which it is connected. I bring this up at this particular point, for if a golfer clearly grasps the interrelationship of the hands, arms, shoulders and hips, he will play good golf—he can't help but play good golf.

ON THE BACKSWING, THE ORDER OF MOVEMENT GOES LIKE THIS: HANDS, ARMS, SHOULDERS, HIPS. (On the downswing the order is just reversed: hips, shoulders, arms, hands.) On the backswing, the hands, arms, and shoulders start to move almost simultaneously.

ACTUALLY, THE HANDS START THE CLUBHEAD BACK A SPLIT SECOND BEFORE THE ARMS START BACK. AND THE ARMS BEGIN THEIR MOVEMENT A SPLIT SECOND BEFORE THE SHOULDERS BEGIN TO TURN. AS A GOLFER ACQUIRES FEEL AND RHYTHM THROUGH PRACTICE, THE HANDS, ARMS AND SHOULDERS WILL INSTINCTIVELY TIE IN ON THIS SPLIT-SECOND SCHEDULE. The main point for the novice is to know that they do start back so closely together that their action is unified.

On the backswing the shoulders are always ahead of the hips as they turn. The shoulders start turning immediately. The hips do not. JUST BEFORE YOUR HANDS REACH HIP LEVEL, THE SHOULDERS, AS THEY TURN, AUTOMATICALLY START PULLING THE HIPS AROUND. AS THE HIPS BEGIN TO TURN, THEY PULL THE LEFT LEG IN TO THE RIGHT. Now let us examine these actions in closer detail.

THE SHOULDERS. You want to turn the shoulders as far around as they'll go. (Your head, of course, remains stationary.) When you have turned your shoulders all the way, your back should face squarely toward your target. (Sam Snead, who is gifted with an unusually supple frame, can turn his back a shade farther around than this. This is fine. The more you can turn your shoulders, the better.) Most golfers think that they make a full shoulder turn going back and they would challenge you if you claimed they didn't, but the truth is that few golfers really complete their shoulder turn. They stop turning when the shoulders are about halfway around; then, in order to get the clubhead all the way back, they break the left arm. This is really a false backswing. It isn't any backswing at all. A golfer can't have control of the club or start down into the ball with any power or speed unless his left arm is straight to begin with. When he bends his left arm, he actually performs only a half swing and he forfeits half his potential power. More than this, he then is led into making many exhausting extra movements that accomplish nothing for him.

An excellent way to check that you are making a full shoulder turn is this: WHEN YOU FINISH YOUR BACK-SWING, YOUR CHIN SHOULD BE HITTING AGAINST THE TOP OF YOUR LEFT SHOULDER. Just where the chin contacts the shoulder depends on the individual golfer's physical proportions. In my own case, it's about an inch from the end of the shoulder. My golf shirts have a worn-down spot at this particular point.

THE HIPS. Turning the hips too soon is an error countless golfers make, and it's a serious error. It destroys your chance of obtaining the power a correctly integrated swing gives you. As you begin the backswing, you must restrain your hips from moving until the turning of the shoulders starts to pull the hips around.

Some prominent golfers advocate taking a big turn with the hips. I don't go along with this. If the hips are turned too far around, then you can create no tension in the muscles between the hips and the shoulders. A golfer wants to have this tension; he wants the mid-section of his body to be tightened up, for this tension is the key to the whole downswing. The downswing, you see, is initiated by turning the hips back to the left. When you have this stored-up tension in the muscles between the hips and the shoulders (and in the muscles of the thighs that work with the hips), you have something with which you can begin the downswing. (This tension will, in fact, automatically help to pull you down into the ball.) As the hips turn back to the left, this turning motion increases their tension. IT IS THIS IN-CREASED TENSION THAT UNWINDS THE UPPER PART OF THE BODY. IT UNWINDS THE SHOULDERS, THE ARMS AND THE HANDS IN THAT ORDER, THE CORRECT ORDER. IT HELPS THE SWING SO MUCH IT MAKES IT ALMOST AUTOMATIC. Your shoulders, arms and hands enter into the swing just when

On the backswing the correct order of
movement is hands, arms, shoulders,
hips. In this sequence the golfer
is shown waggling, returning to
address, and then swinging to the top
of his backswing. Each drawing
emphasizes the parts of the body
which are actively functioning at that
particular stage of the backswing. The
diagram above each drawing denotes
the relative amount of turn of the
shoulders and hips at each of these
progressive stages of the backswing

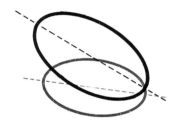

shoulders

hips

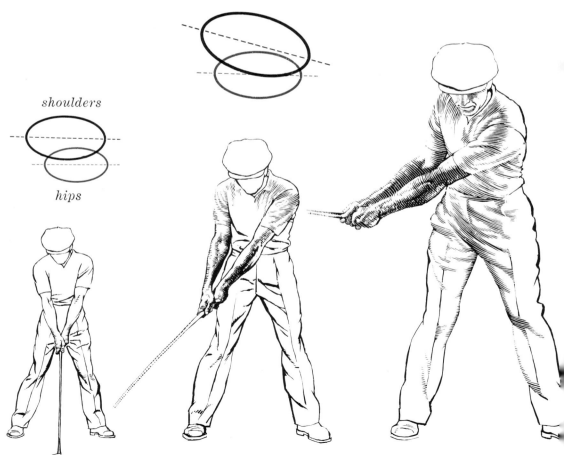

and as they should. They're already loaded with the tension (and power) they've stored up. They're all set to release it.

When the hips are turned back to the left, this tightens the muscles between the hips and the shoulders just a notch more—something like the way a fellow gives each lug that little extra tightening twist when he's changing a tire. Maximum tension in the muscles between the hips and the shoulders produces maximum speed. The tighter the tension in these muscles, the faster the upper part of the body will unwind (as the hips turn) and transfer its speed to the arms and the hands. It gives the upper part of the body a running start. This is the speed that ultimately produces clubhead speed, and clubhead speed is what produces distance.

Now, returning to the backswing, I think you may understand more clearly just why it is so important to have this torsion, this stretching of the muscles, that results from turning your shoulders as far as they can go and retarding the hips. It's the difference in the amount of turn between the shoulders and hips that sets up this muscular tension. If the hips were turned as much as the shoulders, there'd be no tightening up at all.

THE LEGS. When the hips enter the swing, as they are turned they pull the left leg in. The left knee breaks in to the right, the left foot rolls in to the right on the inside part of the sole, and what weight there is on the left leg rides on the inside ball of the foot. LET ME CAUTION YOU AGAINST LIFTING THE LEFT HEEL TOO HIGH OFF THE GROUND ON THE BACKSWING. IF THE HEEL STAYS ON THE GROUND—FINE. IF IT COMES UP AN INCH OFF THE GROUND—FINE. No higher than that, though—it will only lead to faulty balance and other undesirable complications.

The body and the legs move the feet. LET THEM MOVE THE FEET. As regards the left heel, how much the left knee breaks in on the backswing determines how much the heel comes up. I never worry about the left heel. Whether it comes off the ground a half inch or a quarter of an inch or remains on the ground as a result of my body and leg action on the backswing—this is of no importance at all. I pay no attention to it.

As regards the right leg, it should maintain the same position it had at address, the same angle in relation to the ground, throughout the backswing. That is one of the checks the average golfer should make when he's warming up and when he's on the course. When you have a stable right leg and the right knee remains pointed in a bit, it prevents the leg from sagging and swaying out to the right and carrying the body along with it.

There is one other aspect of this first part of the swing that we should take up at this time: the plane. Over the period I've been in golf, oceans of words have been devoted to the arc of the swing but only the merest trickle to the plane. This is unfortunate, for in the dynamics of the golf swing the plane is extremely important, far more important than the arc.

What precisely is this plane? To begin with, there are two planes in the golf swing, the plane of the backswing and

Golfer can check stability of his right leg by marking its angle at address with club, then noting if angle of the club changes when he practices backswing motion

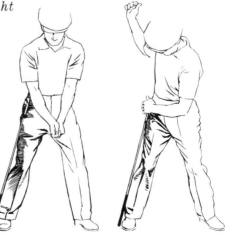

the plane of the downswing. As the drawings will delineate, the plane of the backswing — which is all we will concern ourselves with in this chapter — is most simply described as an angle of inclination running from the ball to the shoulders. The pitch of the angle is determined by two factors: the height of the individual's shoulders and the distance he stands from the ball at address.

On the backswing, the plane serves the golfer as sort of a three-dimensional road map. HIS SHOULDERS SHOULD ROTATE ON THIS PLANE, CONTINUOUSLY INCLINED AT THE SAME ANGLE (WITH THE BALL) THEY ESTABLISHED AT ADDRESS. En route from address to the top of the backswing, THE ARMS AND HANDS (AND THE CLUB) SHOULD ALSO REMAIN ON THIS SAME ANGLE OF INCLINATION AS THEY SWING BACK. (Use your left arm as your guide.) When your shoulders, arms and hands follow the appointed route the plane sets up, it insures you that your upper body and arms will be correctly inter-aligned when they reach that crucial point where the backswing ends and the downswing begins. Then, when the downswing is inaugurated by the hips and the turning hips unwind the upper part of the body, the shoulders and then the arms and then the hands flow easily and powerfully into the swing. In other words, by staying on his backswing plane, the player pre-groups his forces so that each component is correctly geared to work with the other components on the downswing. The energy of the hips, shoulders, arms, and hands will be released in that correct order, and the perfect chain action results. He can put everything he has into the shot. He can obtain maximum distance and accuracy. All powered up to begin with and generating immense power as the downswing accelerates, he has no need to try and manufacture some power somehow with some last-ditch swing-wrecking effort, as poor golfers are forced to do. This kind of misplaced effort produces very little in the way of distance and damages direction left and right. It makes golf a frustrating game—you get so little in return for the energy you put into your shots. However, for the golfer with a correct swing who pre-arranges his chain action by staying on his backswing plane and storing his power properly, golf is a tremendous pleasure. He reaps the full rewards for the effort he pours into it.

There is no such thing as an absolute and standard plane for all golfers. The correct angle for each person's plane depends on how he is built. A fellow whose legs are proportionately shorter than his arms, for example, necessarily creates a shallow angle for his plane. At the other extreme, a man whose legs are proportionately longer than his arms sets up a very steep angle for himself. Neither plane, let me repeat, is incorrect. Technically, it is wrong to term the man who properly swings on a shallow plane a "flat swinger," or the man who properly swings on a steep plane an "upright swinger," simply because their planes happen to be flatter or more upright than the plane of the man of more average proportions. However, if any golfer permits his arms and his club to drop well below his established plane, then, whether he normally possesses a shallow or steep or an average plane, he would be swinging too flat. Similarly, if he hoists his club above the line of his plane, he would be swinging too upright.

Perhaps the best way to visualize what the plane is and how it influences the swing is to imagine that, as the player stands before the ball at address, his head sticks out through a hole in an immense pane of glass that rests on his shoulders as it inclines upward from the ball. IF HE EXECUTES HIS BACKSWING PROPERLY, AS HIS ARMS ARE APPROACHING HIP LEVEL, THEY SHOULD BE PARALLEL WITH THE PLANE AND THEY SHOULD REMAIN PARALLEL WITH THE PLANE, JUST BENEATH THE GLASS, TILL THEY REACH THE TOP OF THE BACKSWING. AT THE TOP OF HIS BACK-

Visualize the backswing plane as a large pane of glass that rests on the shoulders as it inclines upward from the ball. As the arms approach hip level on the backswing, they should be moving parallel with the plane and should remain parallel with the plane [just below the glass] to the top of the backswing. It would be ideal if the arms could be swung back parallel to the plane from the very start of the swing, but because of the way we human beings are constructed, a man gripping a club can't get his arms onto the plane until they are nearly hip high

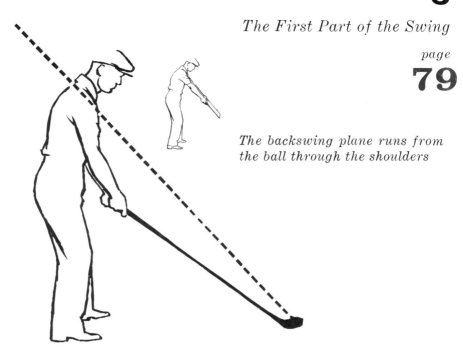

The backswing plane runs from the ball through the shoulders

SWING, HIS LEFT ARM SHOULD BE EXTENDED AT THE EXACT SAME ANGLE (TO THE BALL) AS THE GLASS. Actually, his left arm would brush against the glass. As for his shoulders, as they turn on the backswing, the top of the shoulders will continuously be brushing against the glass.

As golf faults go, it is not too injurious if your club and arms travel on a plane a little flatter than the ideal one. HOWEVER, YOU ARE HEADING FOR DISASTER IF YOU THRUST YOUR ARMS UP ABOVE THE PLANE SO THAT THEY WOULD SHATTER THE PANE OF GLASS. Poor golfers make this error at any and all stages of the backswing, but it occurs most commonly when they are nearing the top of the backswing. Then, when their hands are about shoulder high, they suddenly lift their arms almost vertically towards the sky—crash! goes the glass... and their shot. They conclude the backswing on an entirely different and far more upright plane, with their hands and forearms and elbows pretzeled all over the place. Hopelessly

steep plane

shallow plane

Drawings above and below demonstrate that the arms and club remain below the glass in all stages of backswing

out of position, they struggle to right themselves on the downswing. Invariably, they can't and they mis-hit the ball in every conceivable way and in all directions. There are quite a few fairly talented golfers who also make this mistake of looping their arms above the plane as they approach the top of the backswing. It explains their frequent erratic spells. They cannot groove their compensations, and they make errors on both sides of the fairway.

If you can devote a half hour a day for a week to practicing the backswing I'm sure you will find that you will begin to assimilate the correct movements much more quickly than you think. And you will be far enough advanced to extract maximum profit when we move on to study the second part of the swing.

Practice the waggle—perhaps 10 minutes a day. In this connection, I'd like to add one contingent thought. When the average player gets ready to hit a shot, some days, purely by accident, he does one or two key things correctly. He hasn't the faintest idea what these key things are, but he does them and consequently he plays quite well. On most days, however—on nearly all days, for that matter—he feels very uncomfortable and unconfident as he addresses the ball and he is completely baffled when he tries to figure out the remedies that will give him that sense of rightness. "I just don't have it today," he rationalizes in his bewilderment. "I just can't feel a thing." Well, he's got it that day. If he checks his grip and stance and waggles properly, he'll feel that he's got it and he'll be able to use it.

A second thing I recommend you practice is a training exercise that's designed to school a golfer to entrust his swing not to his hands but to his arms and body. Start in the position of address with the upper part of your arms and your elbows glued to the sides of your chest. Exaggerate this adhesion, if anything. With your arms held as stiff as the pendulum of a clock, have the turning of the body swing the arms back about halfway to the top of the

*The training exercise is a half-swing back and forth. Back
and forth, back and forth, the body swings the arms like a pendulum
of a clock. The elbows remain tightly glued to the sides*

backswing, then swing them forward about halfway to the
finish of the follow-through ... back and forth, back and
forth, breaking your left knee and right elbow on your half-
swing back, breaking your right knee on your halfswing
forward and, later, the left elbow. As you continue to do
this, you will get the feeling that you are swinging with the
hips, that the body is swinging the club. The effect of this
exercise is to exaggerate a fundamental fact and feeling
you want to have about the full golf swing: THE ACTION
OF THE ARMS IS MOTIVATED BY THE MOVE-
MENTS OF THE BODY, AND THE HANDS CON-
SCIOUSLY DO NOTHING BUT MAINTAIN A FIRM
GRIP ON THE CLUB.

Last but not least, practice the complete backswing. Try
to visualize your proper plane and to keep your arms traveling on that plane as you swing the club back. Quite a few
of my friends have told me that once they got the idea of
the plane into their heads, it worked wonders for them. Like
nothing else, it got them out of their old bad habits and
made the correct movements come so naturally they could
hardly believe it.

I can believe it. I really never felt that my own back-swing was satisfactorily grooved, or could be satisfactorily grooved, until I began to base my backswing on this concept of the plane. Up to that time—this was in 1938—I had been struggling along with a backswing that was a lot less uniform and, consequently, a lot less dependable than I wanted it to be. I began to wonder whether or not I could find a set "slot" for the club to hit at the top of the back-swing. Then, if I could swing the club into the slot on every swing—well, that would solve my problem of inconsistency.

I began to think more and more about the golfer's plane. After some experimentation, I found to my enormous relief that, if I swung back along this plane, my club would, in effect, be traveling up a set slot *throughout* my backswing, on swing after swing. If it did that, at the top of the back-swing plane it was bound to hit the end of this set slot, on swing after swing. I practiced swinging on this plane and started to gain confidence that my backswing was reliable. It helped my whole swing, my whole game, my whole attitude. I can honestly say that for the first time I then began to think that I could develop into a golfer of true championship caliber.

4 The Second Part of the Swing

One of the greatest pleasures in golf—I can think of nothing that truly compares with it unless it is watching a well-played shot streak for the flag—is the sensation a golfer experiences at the instant he contacts the ball flush and correctly. He always knows when he does, for then and only then does a distinctive "sweet feeling" sweep straight up the shaft from the clubhead and surge through his arms and his whole frame. Not even the best golfer can hit the ball this well on every shot, for golf, in essence, is a game of misses. Every seasoned, sensible golfer knows this, and, accordingly, he tries to build a swing that is so basically sound that his "misses" are, in truth, not bad golf shots at all —fairly well struck, accurate enough, eminently serviceable.

In this chapter we will be taking up the phase of the swing in which the player actually hits the ball. This second section of the swing—from the start of the downswing to the finish of the follow-through—is the most crucial part, necessarily. This is where everything a player does from the moment he takes his club from the bag either pays off or doesn't. Since, in the method we are teaching, each action is the direct result of preceding actions in the chain-action sequence of the swing, it strikes me that it would be

*The downswing is initiated
by turning the hips to the
left. The shoulders, arms
and hands—in that order—
then release their power.
The great speed developed
in this chain action carries
the golfer all the way
around to the finish
of his follow-through*

extremely profitable, before tackling the downswing, to re-view briefly the plane of the backswing. As we brought out in the last lesson, staying on his plane as he swings back is a golfer's best insurance of being in a correct and powerful position at that critical juncture where his backswing ends and the downswing begins.

As he addresses the ball, the golfer creates the angle of the plane of his backswing: the plane inclines along this imaginary line running from the ball to the top of his shoulders and on upward at that established angle of inclination. If a golfer rotates his shoulders on this plane and swings his arms and club back on this plane—neither dropping them below the plane nor, what is much more disastrous, lifting them above the plane—then at the top of his backswing his left arm will be extended at an angle to the ball identical with the angle of the plane. In terms of functioning, which is more to our point, the shoulders, arms and hands will then be in a perfect position to carry out their interrelated movements on the downswing.

Learning to think in terms of this plane has helped tremendously to improve and stabilize the swings of many friends of mine. Like no other visual suggestion, it seems to induce a golfer to make the correct backswing movements TIME AFTER TIME. He folds the right elbow in, just as he should; his left arm is fully extended but not rigid, just as it should be; he completes his full shoulder turn; his hands cock themselves naturally, without any conscious effort, and the back of his left hand is an unbroken extension of the line of his left wrist and forearm. Not only are his arms and the upper part of his body correctly aligned throughout the backswing, but these various component parts tend to be poised TIME AFTER TIME with the proper degree of live, stretched muscular tension ready to be released on the downswing.

When I am studying and evaluating a golfer's swing, I always make it a point to check how well he adheres to his plane on the backswing. Standing several yards behind him and facing down his line of flight, I slant my forearm and hand (with the fingers extended and joined as in a salute) along the angle of his plane. As he swings back, I can then observe whether or not he stays on the plane throughout his backswing. If he doesn't then I know that this golfer's swing is not soundly constructed and will not be able to repeat under pressure.

On the downswing, a golfer swings on a slightly different plane than on the backswing. THE PLANE FOR THE DOWNSWING IS LESS STEEPLY INCLINED AND IS ORIENTED WITH THE BALL QUITE DIFFERENTLY FROM THE BACKSWING PLANE. The golfer gets on this second plane—without thinking he is changing planes—when he turns his hips back to the left at the start of the downswing. This moves his body to the left and automatically lowers the right shoulder. You will remember that, in introducing the backswing plane, we suggested that the golfer-reader imagine that at address his head is sticking out through a hole in an immense pane of glass that rests on his shoulders as it slants up from the ball. Now, on the downswing, as the body moves to the left and the right shoulder is automatically lowered, this causes the pane of glass to be shifted into a different position. Its lateral axis is no longer in line with the line of flight. It points slightly to the right of the target. (The pane is also tilted so that the leading edge is raised off the ground.) WHEN THE GOLFER IS ON THIS CORRECT DOWNSWING PLANE, HE HAS TO HIT FROM THE INSIDE OUT. When he hits from the inside out, he can get maximum strength into his swing and obtain maximum clubhead speed. Moreover, he has no need to compensate in any way or at any stage of his swing. (Not to get ahead of the story, but if a golfer starts his downswing incorrectly with his shoulders or hands and not with his hips, he cannot get onto the proper plane or hit from the inside out. However, if he starts down correctly by turning his hips,

The backswing plane, as
seen from a top-view
position. At the top of the
backswing, the left arm
should incline at the exact
angle of the plane.
The arm brushes against
the glass pane

The golfer gets on th
downswing plane w
turns his hips to the
to initiate the downs
The plane for the
downswing is inclin
shallower angle tha
plane of the backsw
and its lateral axis p
slightly to the right
of the golfer's targe

To check if a golfer remains on his plane during his backswing, I stand behind him (facing down his line of flight) and slant my forearm and hand along the line of what would be his correct plane. When he swings back, I can then observe whether he stays on his plane, drops below it or lifts his arms above the plane

—— *backswing plane*
—— *downswing plane*

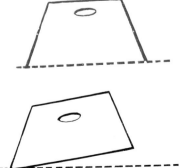
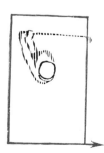

he's all set. He's got to hit from the inside out. He's practically the "captive" of his own good swing.)

While it is dynamically important for a golfer not to depart from his plane at any time during the second part of his swing, being consciously attentive to it does not help him the way a consciousness of his backswing plane promotes a fine, functional backswing. Consequently, my advice would be to know that this downswing plane exists and have it at the back of your mind but to concentrate chiefly on making the one or two key movements which will really do something for you on the downswing.

THE HIPS INITIATE THE DOWNSWING. They are the pivotal element in the chain action. Starting them first and moving them correctly—this one action practically *makes* the downswing. It creates early speed. It transfers the weight from the right foot to the left foot. It takes the hips out of the way and gives your arms plenty of room to pass. It funnels your force forward toward your objective. It puts you in a strong hitting position where the big muscles in the back and the muscles in the shoulders, arms and hands are properly delayed so that they can produce their maximum performance at the right time and place.

To begin the downswing, TURN YOUR HIPS BACK TO THE LEFT. THERE MUST BE ENOUGH LATERAL MOTION FORWARD TO TRANSFER THE WEIGHT TO THE LEFT FOOT. The path the hips take on the downswing is not the exact same path they traveled as they were turned on the backswing. On the downswing, their "arc" should be a trifle wider—both as regards the amount of lateral motion and the amount of eventual rotation around to the rear.

This turning of the hips is activated by several sets of muscles which work together. THE CONTRACTED MUSCLES OF THE LEFT HIP AND THE MUSCLES ALONG THE INSIDE OF THE LEFT THIGH START TO SPIN THE LEFT HIP AROUND TO THE LEFT. AT

ONE AND THE SAME TIME, THE MUSCLES OF THE RIGHT HIP AND THE MUSCLES OF THE RIGHT THIGH—BOTH THE INSIDE AND THE POWERFUL OUTSIDE THIGH MUSCLES—START TO MOVE THE RIGHT HIP FORWARD. In order for them to do this work, these muscles must be stretched taut with tension that is just waiting for the golfer's signal to be released. This tension is built up on the backswing by retarding the hips but rotating the shoulders fully around. If you permit the hips to turn too much on the backswing, this tension and torsion are lost and then there's nothing to start them forward. IMAGINE THAT, AT ADDRESS, ONE END OF AN ELASTIC STRIP IS FASTENED TO A WALL DIRECTLY BEHIND YOUR LEFT HIP AND THAT THE OTHER END IS FASTENED TO YOUR LEFT HIP-BONE. AS THE SHOULDERS TURN THE HIPS ON THE BACKSWING, THE ELASTIC IS STRETCHED WITH INCREASED TENSION. WHEN YOU START TURNING THE HIPS TO THE LEFT, THE ELASTIC WILL SNAP BACK TO THE LEFT WITH TREMENDOUS SPEED. Same thing with the hips. The greater the tension, the faster you can move them. The faster the hips move, the better. They can't go too fast.

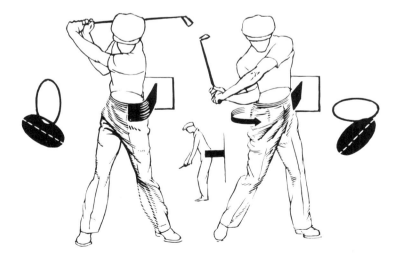

The movement of the hips inaugurates a whole chain of actions. Tied in with the hips, the left leg begins to break back to the left and the left knee turns a bit toward the target. Starting the hips back also takes the pressure off the right leg, and as this happens, the weight flows to the left leg. The right knee breaks in, definitely, toward the target, boosting the mounting velocity of the swing. This is, in truth, what each element does as it joins in the down-swing: IT ADDS ITS CONTRIBUTION TO THE MUL-TIPLYING SPEED GENERATED BY THIS COHESIVE MOVEMENT OF THE BODY, LEGS AND ARMS TOWARD THE TARGET. THIS SPEED MULTIPLIES THE GOLFER'S POWER 10 TIMES OVER. IN THE CHAIN ACTION OF THE SWING, THE SHOULDERS AND UPPER PART OF THE BODY CONDUCT THIS MULTIPLYING POWER INTO THE ARMS...THE ARMS MULTIPLY IT AGAIN AND PASS IT ON TO THE HANDS...THE HANDS MULTIPLY IT IN TURN ...AND, AS A RESULT, THE CLUBHEAD IS SIMPLY TEARING THROUGH THE AIR AT AN INCREDIBLE SPEED AS IT DRIVES THROUGH THE BALL. ALL THIS HAPPENS SO QUICKLY, OF COURSE, THAT YOU CAN'T SEE IT TO APPRECIATE IT. BUT THIS IS WHAT HAPPENS.

The surest way to wreck this remarkable machinery is to start the downswing with the hands instead of with the hips. Nearly all poor players do. By starting down with the hands, they kill their chance for a good shot then and there. They check the rotation of the hips, and if a golfer stops his hip rotation, he's bound to force the whole upper part of his body way outside the proper line. Committed then to bringing the club into the ball from the outside in, he almost invariably slices his shot, for his club has to cut across the proper line. If he doesn't slice, he pulls his shot far to the left as he struggles to offset his usual error. If the average golfer will only start his downswing with his hips, what a world of difference this will make in his swing and his shots, not to mention his score!

Initiating the downswing with the hips is of such critical importance that many top-rung golfers, sensing that their timing will be better accommodated, start to turn their hips to the left a fraction of a second before the club reaches the top of the backswing. There's nothing wrong with this. It amounts to a permissible personal modification and it underlines, if anything, the salient fact that under no condition should the downswing be inaugurated by the hands. Let me put this even more strongly: THE MAIN THING FOR THE NOVICE OR THE AVERAGE GOLFER IS TO KEEP ANY *CONSCIOUS* HAND ACTION OUT OF HIS SWING. THE CORRECT SWING IS FOUNDED ON CHAIN ACTION, AND IF YOU USE THE HANDS WHEN YOU SHOULDN'T, YOU PREVENT THIS CHAIN ACTION.

What *do* the hands do? The answer is they do nothing *active* until after the arms have moved on the downswing to a position just above the level of the hips. The arms don't propel this motion themselves. They are carried down by the movement of the hips. To understand just how the hands and arms get this "free ride," pick up a club, swing it back, and hold your position at the top of the backswing. Now, forgetting about your hands and arms entirely, start to move your hips back to the left, in comparative slow motion. Now look where your hands are. This movement of the hips has automatically carried them down from the top —quite a good ways down, in fact, so that they are just about at hip level. In this position, tied in as they are with the body's ever-building speed and power, the arms and hands should feel absolutely loaded with power. Everything you did from the grip on was calculated to get you into this position. You cannot simulate this position or arrive at it by leaving out one of the integrated steps. Only if they have carried out the fundamental movements will the correct

The turning of the hips
inaugurates the downsw
This movement of the h
automatically lowers th
arms and hands to a pos
just above hip level

en he has inaugurated
downswing by turning
hips, a golfer suddenly
omes aware of his
mendous stored-up power

parts of the body be correctly interpoised at this critical time in the swing to pick up this terrific load of energy and deliver it.

AFTER YOU HAVE INITIATED THE DOWNSWING WITH THE HIPS, YOU WANT TO THINK OF ONLY ONE THING: HITTING THE BALL. On a full drive, I try to hit the ball hard, sometimes as hard as I can. On other shots where the premium on distance is not so high, I try to hit the ball as hard as the particular shot warrants. I don't give as much as a passing thought to how the face of my club will contact the ball. That's all been taken care of before, at address and during the waggle. Consciously trying to control the face of the club at impact is folly. You cannot time such a delicate and devilish thing. It happens too fast, much too fast.

As I explain to my audiences at golf clinics, the correct hitting motion is one unbroken thrust from the beginning of the downswing to the end of the follow-through. I point out also that I think of only two things: starting the hips back and then hitting just as hard as I can with the upper part of my body, my arms and my hands, in that order. When I expound this one-piece hit-through action, I generally experience two main types of reactions from the members of a clinic audience. The first is a kind of polite skepticism which might be put into words like this: "I bet there's more to it. Nothing could be that simple. There has to be more conscious technique at impact. That's the inside dope which the pros never tell us outsiders." The second type of reaction is sort of a misguided cynicism which might go something like this: "Sure, if you're a pro and have practically eaten your lunch on the practice tee for 20 years, then, maybe, everything has become so second nature that you don't have to think of anything but hitting through with all your beef. Hogan's explanation of what he does is O.K. for Hogan, but it will probably do us average golfers as much good as if Bob Richards were to tell us that pole-vaulting is really nothing at all—once you have pushed off from your pole and are 14 feet or so in the air, all you have to do is to roll over the bar, neatly." I can understand these reactions but they are simply not accurate reflections of the facts. I would not be undertaking these lessons, for example, if I were not genuinely convinced that the average golfer has the requisite physical ability to use the same methods fundamentally that all the top golfers use. The average golfer's problem is not so much a lack of ability as it is a lack of knowing what he should do.

Once a player reaches that phase of the downswing where his hands are at about the level of his hips—the start of the impact segment of the swing, we might term it—if he has performed the swing correctly up to that point, he is so set up that he instinctively hits through the ball and follows through correctly. You can't keep from doing it right. It helps a golfer, nonetheless, to have a clear idea of what the arms and the hands actually do during this climactic part of the swing. Then he can practice these movements,

In its general character, the correct motion of the right arm and hand in the impact area resembles the motion an infielder makes when he throws half sidearm, half underhand to first after fielding a ground ball. As the right arm swings forward, the right elbow is very close to the right hip and "leads" the arm—it is the part of the arm nearest target

*As in the old two-hand
basketball pass, the left arm
and hand lead the right
arm and hand. Be sure you
hit through with the left
as hard as with the right*

and if he practices them intelligently, he is certain to improve his skill in executing them.

Let us first study the correct motion of the right arm and hand in the impact area. It has always seemed to me that, in its general character, this motion is quite similar to the one an infielder makes when he throws half underhand, half sidearm to first after scooping up a ground ball. As he swings his arm forward, his right elbow is very close to his right hip. The elbow "leads" the arm—it is the part of the arm nearest the target as he begins to make the throw. The forearm and hand catch up with the elbow, and the player's arm is extended relatively straight when he releases the

ball. As he follows through, the wrist and hand gradually turn over, and his palm faces the ground at the finish of his follow-through.

On a full shot you want to hit the ball as hard as you can with your right hand. But this is only half the story. HIT THE BALL AS HARD AS YOU CAN WITH BOTH HANDS. The left is a power hand, too. If you hit hard with only the right and let the left go to sleep, you will not only lose much valuable power, you also will run into all the errors that result when the right hand overpowers the left. YOU MUST HIT AS HARD WITH THE LEFT AS WITH THE RIGHT.

What is the correct integrated motion the two arms and hands make as they approach the ball and hit through it? What does it feel like as it is happening? Well, if there is any motion in sports which it resembles, it is the old two-handed basketball pass, from the right side of the body. As the player enters the impact area and the hands start to pass the right hip, it is almost as if his hands were holding a ball as they move toward the target, the left arm and hand leading, the right arm and hand following—positioned just the way they are on the shaft. The ball is about the size of the two hands. It is a heavy ball, heavy in the way a small-sized medicine ball would be. It takes muscle to throw it hard. Straight ahead of the player, maybe four or five yards ahead down his line of flight, stands a fairly large target. The center of the target is about the same height from the ground as the player's belt buckle. As he shifts his weight from his right foot to his left to get all his power into his throw, the player flings the ball at the target just as hard as he can, whipping the ball with both arms and both hands, since he can throw it harder and more accurately that way. He wants that ball to travel on a line and smash into the center of the target so emphatically that it will knock the bull's-eye right off it. (The forcefulness of this effort carries the player all the way around in his follow-through.)

The great value, as I see it, of thinking in terms of this joint two-hand action is that it keeps the left hand driving all the time. During this climactic part of the swing, the left wrist and the back of the left hand begin to supinate very slightly—that is, to turn from a position where the palm is down to a position where the palm is up. They continue to supinate throughout the rest of the swing. The sequence drawings on page 102 describe the exact nature of this gradual supination much more clearly than words can.

In the sequence, there is one position of such signal importance that it warrants closeup study. This is the position of the left wrist and hand at the actual moment of impact.

AT IMPACT THE BACK OF THE LEFT HAND FACES TOWARD YOUR TARGET. THE WRIST BONE IS DEFINITELY RAISED. IT POINTS TO THE TARGET AND, AT THE MOMENT THE BALL IS CONTACTED, IT IS OUT IN FRONT, NEARER TO THE TARGET THAN ANY PART OF THE HAND. When the left wrist is in this position, the left hand will not check or interrupt the speed with which your clubhead is traveling. There's no danger either that the right hand will overpower the left and twist the club over. It can't. As far as applying power goes, I wish that I had three right hands!

Every good golfer has his left wrist in this supinating position at impact. Every poor golfer does the exact reverse. As his club comes into the ball, he starts to pronate the left wrist—to turn it so that the palm will be facing down.

When a golfer's left wrist begins to pronate just before impact, it changes his arc: it shortens it drastically and makes the pitch of his upswing altogether too steep and constricted. At the very point in the swing in which he should be increasing the speed of his hands, by pronating he slows them down. Instead of accelerating and picking up speed on the way down and having great speed at impact, he has expended all his speed before he hits the ball. Letting the left wrist and hand pronate brings on a multitude of other things, none of them good. By changing his arc and plane, for example, the poor player frequently catches the ball too low on the blade and skulls it, or he hits back of the ball. If the face of the club is open, he gets a big scoop slice. If it's closed, he pulls as well as hooks—the ball never starts on its intended line. By pronating, in short, he never has a chance to get that "sweet feeling." It's just impossible.

The downswing arc of the golfer who pronates practically retraces the pattern of his backswing arc, and the down-

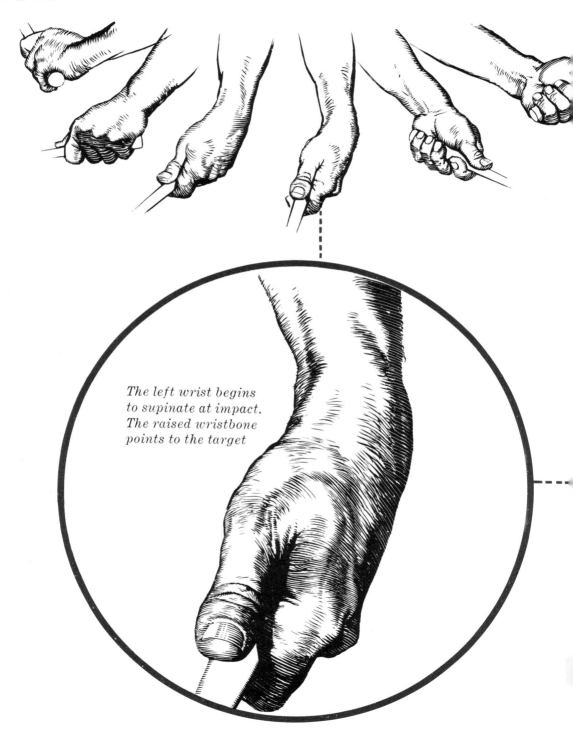

The left wrist begins
to supinate at impact.
The raised wristbone
points to the target

*By pronating his left wrist
just before impact, a
golfer expends his clubhead
speed before he strikes
the ball, restricts the arc
of his swing, opens
himself to making
numerous other errors*

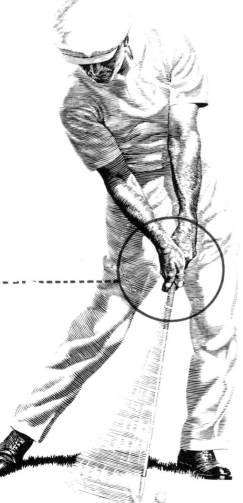

incorrect arc

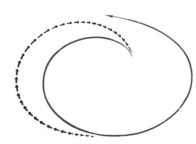

correct arc

swing should not be a retrace of the backswing. Supinating, on the other hand, sets up a number of extremely desirable actions. It helps the player to develop a properly wide forward arc. It puts him in a position where his arms are well extended at impact and will be fully extended just after impact as they swing out toward his objective. The wider his arc, the more room he has in which to build up clubhead speed, the prime factor behind distance.

Supination builds distance and accuracy in other ways. For one thing, it helps you to strike the ball absolutely clean, before the club takes turf. (This is why when you see a good pro hit a ball, there is a real sweet crack at contact and the ball takes off like a bullet. If you first contact the ball right, then almost automatically you'll take turf right, past the ball.) Second, since this slight supination action places the hands a shade ahead of the clubhead at impact, some loft is subtracted from the face of the club. (That's why you marvel at the distance topnotch players can hit the ball. They actually turn a five-iron into a four-iron. The pronating golfer does just the opposite. He increases the loft of his blade. He makes a seven-iron out of his five-iron.)

Every good golfer supinates his left wrist. It is a "must." Of all the players I've seen, Jimmy Demaret undoubtedly emphasizes this action the most. You can't supinate the left wrist more pronouncedly than Jimmy does. When you watch Demaret, you get the feeling that he is really lashing the ball with the back of his left hand. It goes a long way to explain Jimmy's longevity as a first-class player, not to mention his ability to play the ball low and control it under very windy conditions that blow other men all over the course. This supination action, it should be added, also enables you to get maximum grip, maximum backspin on the ball. It is the explanation behind the most amazing shot in the modern pro's repertoire: the low-flying wedge that looks like it was skulled but which bites immediately when it hits the green and then spins itself out close to where it landed.

When you are playing chips, pitches, trap shots and other strokes near and around the green, the hands should function the same as they do on a full swing. With the obvious exception of the explosion trap shot, remember that you contact the ball first. Hit the ball on the downswing and hit right on through the ball. The club face supplies the loft. Supination helps you supply a correct stroke: not a downward chop or an upward scoop but a golf swing with as much coordination as a full shot.

There are a few other points related to the impact area and the follow-through that we should discuss now. Most of these points concern themselves with correct positions —positions which a good golfer moves into naturally if he starts his downswing by turning his hips and then simply hits through to the finish of his swing in one unified motion. As you practice, don't try to force yourself into these positions. They're part and parcel of the chain action. You'll move into them if you execute the fundamentals properly. By touching on these points, though, I think we can clear up quite a few popular misconceptions about the golf swing and implant more firmly correct positive ideas that you can use as guides and check points as you practice and play.

To start with, most golfers—whether or not they actually achieve it in their swings—have the mistaken idea that at the moment of impact both arms should be straightened out their full length. This, of course, isn't right. AT IMPACT THE RIGHT ARM IS STILL BENT SLIGHTLY. On the downswing the right arm gradually straightens out as it comes into the ball, but it isn't until the clubhead is two feet or so past the ball that it straightens out completely. At this point, the left arm is also straight—the one and only time in the swing that both arms are fully extended. After this, led by the supinating left wrist, the left arm begins to fold in at the elbow, like the right arm does on the backswing. As for the right arm, it remains straight, right on through to the finish of the swing, as the left arm does on the back-

*On the downswing the correct order of movement is hips,
shoulders, arms and hands. As each component part enters the
swing, it adds its contribution to the multiplying speed
generated by this cohesive chain-action movement to the left*

page
106

swing. At the finish of the swing—again this is like the
backswing reversed—the left elbow points directly to the
ground, and the top of the player's right shoulder hits up
against his chin. My chin hits the shoulder about an inch
from the end of the shoulder.

AT THAT POINT JUST BEYOND IMPACT WHERE
BOTH ARMS ARE STRAIGHT AND EXTENDED THE
CLUBHEAD REACHES ITS MAXIMUM SPEED—not
at impact. This terrific speed carries the golfer right on
around in that big high finish. At the completion of his
swing, the player's belt buckle does not point directly at
his target. It should point definitely to the left of his target.
If he has gotten all the way through and around with his
hips, the hipbones should be squared to the front. THE
HIPS LEAD THE SHOULDERS ALL THE WAY ON

THE DOWNSWING. The shoulders finally catch up with the hips at the end of the swing.

As regards the legs, a great many golfers think that classical style prescribes that, at impact and throughout the follow-through, the left leg should be as straight as a stick. Definitely not. If you keep your left leg straight, you prohibit your hips from making their full turn and restrict the whole free flow of your body to the left. When your weight doesn't get sufficiently transferred to the left, your arc is cramped, and your body, arms and hands cannot release the full power they're capable of pouring into the shot.

On a good swing, when the player's hands are approaching hip level on the downswing, his hips have already reached that point in their turn when they have begun to open—to face down the fairway. (The belt buckle, when the hands are hip high, is about in line with the ball.) The two legs respond to the hip turn on the downswing. The left leg breaks resiliently to the left, and as the bulk of the weight rides forward to the left side of the left foot, the leg bows out toward the target. As for the right leg, as we pointed out earlier, it breaks in at the knee as the hip turn starts.

When you're practicing this lesson, I suggest you spend some time reviewing the backswing plane and devote perhaps a half hour daily to the hip turn and the hit-through movements. Don't be afraid of swinging too hard. Many golfers are, you know. They figure that unless they restrain their power, they'll magnify their errors. I see it just the other way. If you are working with muscles that are fully extended on swing after swing, there has to be more uniformity than if your muscles are flexed with varying degrees of tension and so "give" differently on one swing and another.

I feel, and I have proved to myself, that I can hit a ball straighter if I hit it hard and full. As a matter of fact, when he is playing a long and testing course, a golfer who has a sound swing wouldn't mind at all having the physique of a giant. The more power he had at his command, the better he'd feel about it. He'd know how to use it. He'd be so long he'd be shooting back at the greens!

5 Summary and Review

The material presented in this book, as I said at the beginning, amounts to a sifting of the knowledge I have picked up during my 25 years as a professional golfer. I am hopeful that these lessons will accomplish two things. First, I trust they will greatly increase the average player's enjoyment of this incredibly fascinating game by enabling him to become a real golfer with a sound, powerful, repeating swing. I feel sure they will do this for any player who gains a clear understanding of the fundamental movements (which we went into in the first four lessons) and who will then continue to practice and familiarize himself with these fundamentals throughout this golf season. In this final chapter we will be putting the whole swing together as we review these modern fundamentals of golf.

And second—I hope that these lessons will serve as a body of knowledge that will lead to further advances in our understanding of the golf swing. Every year we learn a little more about golf. Each new chunk of valid knowledge paves the way to greater knowledge. Golf is like medicine and the other fields of science in this respect. In another 15 years, just as there will be many new discoveries in medicine based on and made possible by present-day strides, we will similarly have refined and extended our present-day knowledge of golf. A golfer, as I see it, has 15 or 20 really productive years—years in which his efforts to realize his full potential as a golfer lead him to speculate about and experiment with every phase of technique, continuously and intensively. He can only find out so much. There are only so many days in a week and only so much daylight in a day. Had I, as a young man starting out in professional golf in 1931, known then what I have managed to learn by 1957 and been able to start my experimentation at this more advanced point, I would have been privileged to have pos-

I find it is helpful if I jot down after practicing exactly what I have been working on and precisely how it was coming along

sibly made more advanced contributions during my best productive years. Other younger men will have that immense pleasure and privilege.

I was thinking the other day, "What a long time I have been learning about golf!" I must have been about 13 when I started to work on my game conscientiously. I was caddying then at the Glen Garden club in Fort Worth, and I took a member named Ed Stewart as my model. A very fine amateur, Stewart was a workingman who couldn't afford to play too often, and none of the other boys wanted to become his regular caddy. That suited me fine. I caddied for him whenever he played and studied his swing and his shotmaking technique closely. Then I'd go and compare my swing with his and try to improve mine by copying certain of Stewart's movements that were obviously correct and desirable.

The first really important change I effected was the action of my left knee. Mine used to shoot straight out when I took the club back. Ed Stewart's knee, I noticed, broke in nicely to the right. I practiced correcting my knee action on the lawn at home until there was no lawn left. In the neighborhood where our family lived, each of the houses had a small lawn that was separated from the others by hedges. The grocery store was about six houses or six lawns away. Whenever my mother sent me to the store for a loaf of bread or a pound of butter or whatever it was, I never walked to the store, I always played to it, sometimes chipping from one lawn to the next, sometimes setting the lawn two or three hedges away as my "green," sometimes hitting to the farthest "green" with a full nine-iron shot — all the time checking my left knee action or whatever phase of my swing I was working on. I doubt if my practice improved the looks of the neighborhood, but it was awfully good for my game.

In golf, you know, you learn some things very early and other things surprisingly late. For example, take just three of the several elements I now regard as absolutely fundamental to any and every good swing: the proper waggle, the proper hip turn, and the proper backswing plane. I came to understand the value of the waggle comparatively early: I was just starting to follow the circuit in 1932 when I learned from observing Johnny Revolta and talking with him that this genius of the short game geared himself for the different demands of each shot around the greens by modifying his waggle to suit that particular shot. Say he had to pop the ball over a bunker and have it put on the brakes immediately. He'd waggle with sharp, staccato, jabby strokes, a "coming attraction" of the stroke he'd use to clip the ball the way it had to be clipped to produce maximum bite. Or say he was pitching the ball to land on a selected point on a slippery green and was going to let the ball trickle the rest of the way to the cup down a side slope. He'd gear himself then with delicate, little pencil-stroke waggles that seemed to be all finger tips. And so on and on—an individual waggle for each different chip shot in his marvelous repertoire. It struck me that it would be a very intelligent thing to use this method of Johnny's not only for my short shots but to adapt it also for my full shots. I began to do so immediately.

Not long after this—in the middle 1930s, I would say—I got the correct hip-turn action clear in my mind, mainly from studying newsreel movies of the best golfers in action. It wasn't until 1938, though, that I grasped the concept of the plane. I'd been thinking sporadically about the plane for some time before that, examining the plane on which the batter swings in baseball and making some tentative suppositions about the golfer's plane. Yet it wasn't until I really began to worry about the unreliability of my backswing that I was driven to conduct a serious investigation of the plane. Long before I fully understood what the plane did for you and why it worked out that way, I realized that I had hit on something of tremendous significance for me.

On the winter circuit, as we traveled from tournament to tournament, I would be up in my hotel room night after night studying my backswing plane in the full-length mirror, trying to memorize it so well I would instinctively swing back the same way time after time.

In the seasons before the war, as I learned more and more about the golf swing and how to play golf, I enjoyed increasing success on the tournament circuit. Nevertheless, I never felt genuinely confident about my game until 1946. Up to that year, while I knew once I was on the course and playing well that I had the stuff that day to make a good showing, before a round I had no idea whether I'd be 69 or 79. I felt my game might suddenly go sour on any given morning. I had no assurance that if I was a little off my best form I could still produce a respectable round. My friends on the tour used to tell me that I was silly to worry, that I had a grooved swing and had every reason to have confidence in it. But my self-doubting never stopped. Regardless of how well I was going, I was still concerned about the next day and the next day and the next.

In 1946 my attitude suddenly changed. I honestly began to feel that I could count on playing fairly well each time I went out, that there was no practical reason for me to feel I might suddenly "lose it all." I would guess that what lay behind my new confidence was this: I had stopped trying to do a great many difficult things perfectly because it had become clear in my mind that this ambitious over-thoroughness was neither possible nor advisable, or even necessary. All you needed to groove were the fundamental movements—and there weren't so many of them. Moreover, they were movements that were basically controllable and so could be executed fairly well whether you happened to be sharp or not so sharp that morning. I don't know what came first, the chicken or the egg, but at about the same time I began to feel that I had the stuff to play creditable golf even when I was not at my best, my shot making

started to take on a new and more stable consistency. THE BASIS FOR THIS PROGRESS, LET ME REPEAT, WAS MY GENUINE CONVICTION THAT ALL THAT IS REALLY REQUIRED TO PLAY GOOD GOLF IS TO EXECUTE PROPERLY A RELATIVELY SMALL NUMBER OF TRUE FUNDAMENTAL MOVEMENTS.

Now that we have gone into the swing, stage by stage, from the grip to the finish, I think it would be extremely instructive to "wind the swing back" and see what are the key fundamental actions a golfer performs to move correctly from one position to another.

To begin with, what does a golfer do to arrive at the correct position at the finish of his swing?

As we have said, the follow-through is not the result of any specific new actions in the last stages of the swing. The proper chain-action movement plus the clubhead speed it builds carry the golfer all the way through to a perfect finish. The golfer is bound to follow through correctly, PROVIDED HE COMES INTO THE BALL AND HITS THROUGH THE BALL CORRECTLY.

All right, then. What are the major things a golfer must do to be correctly poised and positioned as he hits through the ball?

He will be essentially correct in the impact area if he learns to execute three major movements. 1) He must initiate the downswing by turning the hips to the left. 2) He must hit through to the finish of his swing in one cohesive movement, hitting with his hips, shoulders, arms and hands, in that order. 3) He must start to supinate his left wrist just before impact. This is, essentially, all he need concentrate on, PROVIDED HE IS IN THE CORRECT POSITION AT THE TOP OF HIS BACKSWING.

How does a golfer get himself to this correct position at the top of the backswing?

He will be essentially correct when he arrives at the top

of his backswing if he 1) waggles properly; 2) starts back with his hands, arms and shoulders and lets his shoulders turn his hips; and 3) stays on his plane throughout his backswing. These are all the movements he has to work on during his backswing, PROVIDED HE IS CORRECTLY POSITIONED AND POISED AT ADDRESS.

And, finally, what makes up this correct position at address? The answer, of course, is a correct stance and posture and a correct grip.

Now, that isn't so many key fundamental movements to remember and work on. I believe it comes to eight. The whole swing starts with the grip and builds from there. Each correct movement is linked with and sets up the next ensuing movement. The whole swing is chain action.

When a certain phase of your swing is not functioning properly, I would suggest that you refresh your knowledge of that particular phase (by rereading the pertinent pages in the earlier chapters) and then working things out on the practice tee. AND WHETHER YOU ARE PRACTICING OR PLAYING, SCHOOL YOURSELF TO THINK IN TERMS OF THE CAUSE AND NOT THE RESULT. Let me illustrate what I mean by this. Say a golfer picks his head up and mis-hits his shot badly. His partner will usually tell him, "You didn't keep your head down," as if this were the true cause of his poor shot. It isn't. The true cause was some faulty movement in the golfer's swing that made him pull his head up. For example, if the golfer starts down from the top with his shoulders or his hands and not with his hips, he can't possibly hold his head where it should be. If you are swinging correctly, on the other hand, you can't look at anything but the ball.

Let us briefly review now some of the significant positions and movements that you would do well to practice and check as you work to build a correct, powerful, repeating swing.

The Grip

Left Hand

Place the club so that the shaft is pressed up under the muscular pad of the heel and also lies across top joint of the forefinger. The main pressure points are the last three fingers and the heel pad. The V should point to right eye

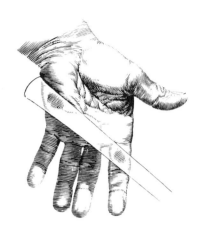

Right Hand

A finger grip. The shaft should lie across top joint of the fingers, definitely below palm. The two middle fingers apply most of the pressure. Practice with the thumb and the forefinger off the shaft. The V points directly to the chin

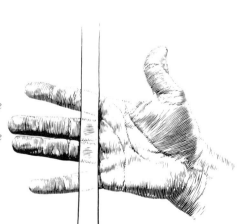

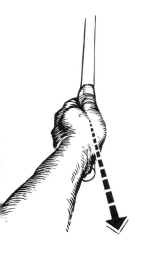

Completed Grip

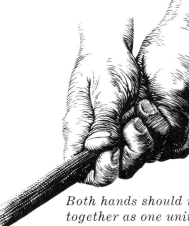

Both hands should work
together as one unit.
The little finger of the right
hand locks into the groove
between forefinger and big
finger of left. The left
thumb should fit snuggly
into the cup of right palm

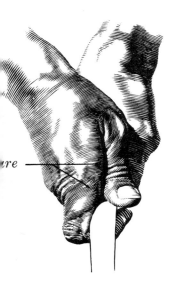

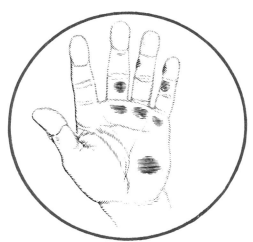

diagram showing correct location of calluses

*There is one correct basic stance:
the right foot is square to the line,
the left foot is pointed out a quarter
turn. On a five-iron, the feet should
be set apart the width of the shoulders.
The stance widens for the longer
clubs, narrows for shorter clubs.
It is extremely important to keep the
elbows and the arms as close
together as possible.
Remember, too: the knees point in*

*When you bend the knees,
upper trunk remains erect*

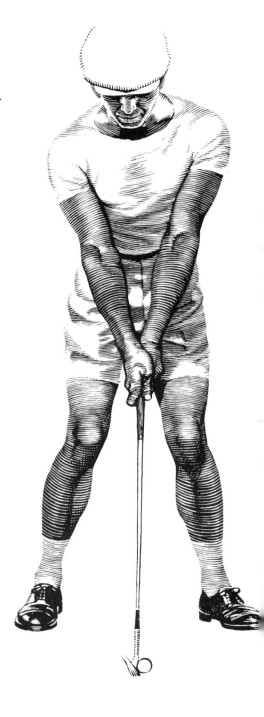

*Right elbow should point
directly to the right hip*

*Left elbow should point
directly to the left hip*

*Correct stance will govern
proper amount of hip turn*

The First Part
of the Swing

The Plane.

*Backswing plane
inclines upward from the
ball through the shoulders.
As arms approach hip level
on backswing, they should
be moving parallel with
the plane and should remain
parallel with the plane
throughout the backswing*

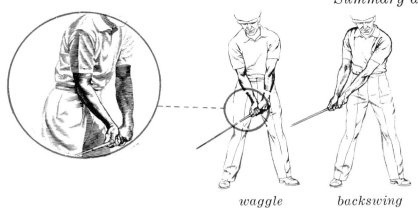

waggle   backswing

The Waggle.

When the player waggles
the club back, right elbow
should hit the front part
of the right hip. As the
lower part of his left arm
rotates on the back waggle,
the golfer actually gets
on backswing plane

r of Movement.

hands, arms and
ulders start the club
k almost simultaneously.
the shoulders turn,
start to turn the hips.
rect tension in the
cles between shoulders
hips created by
rding hip turn

ders

os

The Second Part of the Swing

shoulders

hips

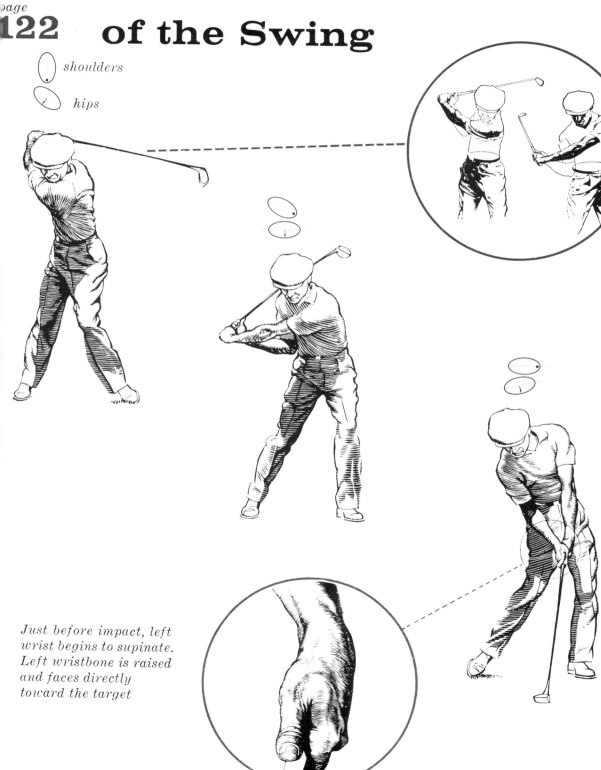

Just before impact, left wrist begins to supinate. Left wristbone is raised and faces directly toward the target

*The turning of the hips back to the left
initiates the downswing. (As pictured
at the left, this movement of the
hips automatically lowers the arms
and the hands to a position just
above the level of the hips.) In the
chain action of the downswing,
the hips are the pivotal element.
The turning of the hips to the left
releases the body, legs and arms in a
cohesive movement to the left.
As it enters the swing, each component
adds its contribution to the
ever-increasing speed and power of
the swing. In this chain action, the
shoulders and the upper part of the
body conduct the multiplying power
into the arms. The arms multiply
it again and pass it on to the hands.
The hands multiply it in turn.
As a result, the clubhead is simply
tearing through the air at an
incredible speed as the golfer hits
through the ball*

The golf swing we have presented in these lessons is the essential golf swing, stripped down to its authentic fundamentals. They are all the golfer needs in order to develop a correct, powerful swing that will repeat. If he learns to execute these fundamental movements—and there is no movement in this swing which a man or woman of average coordination cannot perform—he will continue to become a more and more skillful player. He will not have to worry constantly about his timing, for example, as does the player who thinks he can construct a swing on hand action and who, since this is impossible, is doomed to be erratic. The golfer whose swing is founded on chain action cannot help but have timing. The swing is already timed for him. The chain action itself is the timing.

There is another basic virtue and value in this method we have presented: the golfer has to learn only one swing. HE USES THE SAME FUNDAMENTAL SWING FOR EVERY SHOT HE PLAYS. On all standard shots the ball should be spotted in the same position relative to the left foot. (I spot it a half inch to an inch inside the left heel, toward the right foot.) You can, to be sure, play the ball a shade farther forward or back—it varies from individual to individual, depending on the spot that is the lowest point in his swing. In any event, the relative position of the left foot and the ball remains constant. When you narrow the width of the stance to accommodate the shorter shafts of the irons, you do this by moving the right foot progressively closer to the left foot and toward the ball.

Whether you are playing a full driver or a five-iron or a wedge, you make no conscious variation in the way you perform your swing. Without your knowing it, your swing will change slightly as the length of the shaft of the club changes. (My driver, for example, is 43 inches long; my two-iron, $38\frac{1}{2}$ inches; my five, 37 inches; my wedge, $34\frac{1}{2}$ inches.) The shorter the shaft, the closer the player must stand to the ball. His plane accordingly becomes more upright and the length of his arc is naturally shortened.

When you shorten your arc, you have less time on your swing to get your left hip out of the way. That is why I make—and suggest you make—a mild modification when you are playing the clubs from the six-iron down to the wedge: GET THE LEFT HIP OUT OF THE WAY BEFORE YOU BEGIN TO PLAY YOUR STROKE. You do this by setting your right foot a bit nearer the ball at address, as the diagram below illustrates.

This has the effect of drawing the left foot back from the direct line and turning the left hip a bit to the left—opening the hip a shade, in other words. When you play the clubs from the six-iron down with your body in this position, you still feel like you're taking a full swing. Actually you're not. You have placed a further restriction on the length of your arc. You will sacrifice some distance as a result—the club cannot travel so fast on a shorter arc—but what you lose in distance you more than make up for in direction. When you're playing the short irons, accuracy, of course, is the primary consideration.

The golfer-reader who has applied himself with some

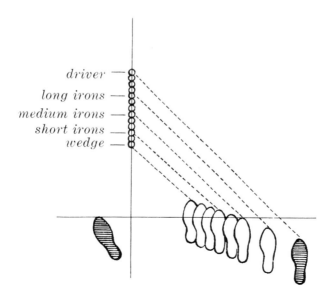

driver
long irons
medium irons
short irons
wedge

diligence to these lessons, spending at least a week on each, should already be well on his way to developing a correct, repeating swing. However, you cannot expect to acquire a real control of the correct movements in a month's time. You must continue to work on these fundamentals throughout the golf season, both on the course and on the practice tee. Through this steady familiarization you will gradually come to execute the movements of the swing more easily and more efficiently. Within six months—as soon as that—an average golfer who has applied himself intelligently should be coming close to breaking 80 or actually break 80. And he will find that he will continue to improve, which is the greatest pleasure of all.

The familiarization that the golfer will gain over the course of just one season of abiding by and practicing the fundamentals will begin to make the correct movements second nature for him. The more he can trust his swing to muscle memory, the more attention he can then turn to managing his golf—that is, thinking out the proper strategy for playing each hole, deciding which of the alternate routes to the pin is the wise one under the immediate conditions, playing the right kind of shot to suit the terrain and the elements, meeting, in short, the ever-fresh challenge which a fine golf hole presents to a man who understands the game and has the necessary equipment to play it well.

I have always thought of golf as the best of all games— the most interesting, the most demanding, the most rewarding. I cannot begin to express the gratification I have always felt in being a part of a game with such a wonderful flavor and spirit, a game which has produced such superb champions and attractive personalities as Harry Vardon, Francis Ouimet, Bob Jones, Walter Hagen, Gene Sarazen, Tommy Armour, Sam Snead, Byron Nelson, Jimmy Demaret—to name only a few of the great players. I have found

Summary and Review

the game to be, in all factualness, a universal language wherever I traveled at home or abroad. I have really enjoyed every minute I have spent in golf—above all, the many wonderful friends I have made. I have loved playing the game and practicing it. Whether my schedule for the following day called for a tournament round or merely a trip to the practice tee, the prospect that there was going to be golf in it made me feel privileged and extremely happy, and I couldn't wait for the sun to come up the next morning so that I could get out on the course again.